Thanks!

Ros.

SACRED COWS

SACRED COWS

IS FEMINISM RELEVANT
TO THE NEW MILLENNIUM?

Rosalind Coward

HarperCollins*Publishers*

HarperCollins*Publishers*
77–85 Fulham Palace Road,
Hammersmith, London w6 8jb

Published by HarperCollins*Publishers* 1999
9 8 7 6 5 4 3 2 1

A catalogue record for this book is
available from the British Library

ISBN 0 00 255551 4

Set in Baskerville by
Rowland Phototypesetting Ltd,
Bury St Edmunds, Suffolk

Printed and bound in Great Britain by
Caledonian International Book Manufacturing Ltd, Glasgow

ACKNOWLEDGEMENTS

This book would not have been written without the support and encouragement of certain friends and colleagues. So, without blaming them, I would like to thank the following people: Karen Binks, Karen Selby, Judy Holder, and Tessa Adams. Jo Dobry, Julian LeVay and Ann McFerran deserve especial thanks for their refusal to let me give up on the project. I would like to acknowledge Barbara Taylor for her ongoing contribution to formulating some of the ideas and more specially for her collaboration with an original version of the chapter, Whipping Boys. Ruth Glaister also gave practical support at a critical moment. I would also like to acknowledge various editors at the *Guardian*, especially David Rowan, David Leigh and Sally Weale for giving me space to develop ideas and sometimes for ruthlessly challenging them. I owe thanks to Michael Fishwick at HarperCollins and Antony Goff at David Higham Associates for their incredible patience. I would also like to thank my Mother for her continuing support and her invaluable cuttings service. Finally I would like to thank John Ellis. Quite simply, without his support this book would never have been written.

CONTENTS

INTRODUCTION

Feminism has been a dramatically successful social movement. It has utterly changed what women can expect from, or do with, their lives. It has also transformed what men expect from sharing their lives with women and how they will behave towards them. Children growing up now simply take for granted feminism's messages about sexual equality and justice when only thirty years ago such messages were widely opposed as extremist and threatening to the social order. No other social movement has so rapidly revolutionized such deeply held patterns of behaviour. The problems faced by feminism now have nothing to do with getting its ideas across and everything to do with how to face up to the unpredictable consequences of this success.

Paradoxically, however, as an increasing number of feminists reach ever more powerful positions, they seem determined to breathe new life into the original tenets of feminism, insisting that female oppression is just as real now as ever before. In the UK and America there are powerful feminists in government who call on the female populace to back them up in a continuing struggle. 'At last', they seem to say, 'you have someone to take up your cause, to fight for women's rights. And what a hard fight it will be because nothing has really changed.' Recently I told a well-known, highly paid woman novelist the sub-title of this book: 'Is feminism relevant to the new millennium?' 'Of course it is,' she said without missing a beat. 'We still don't have equal pay.' Everywhere, powerful women repeat this mantra. Even Germaine Greer now says nothing has really changed. Influential feminists insist that because there are still many individual areas of injustice or unfairness, there is still an

1

overarching system of sexual injustice with men always advantaged and women disadvantaged. One injustice, like the inequality which exists between the average pay of women and the average pay of men, is supposed to prove the rest. But this is no longer true in any simple way. Of course, women still suffer many injustices, discriminations and sometimes even outrages but it is no longer a simple coherent picture of male advantage and female disadvantage.

There are many social practices and attitudes which still discriminate against women. I encounter this regularly in my own life as a journalist and in the media. In these areas, men still tend to dominate. They are still more interested in each other and in each other's interests than in women – a sort of unconscious marginalization which women have long noticed in business. It is still more difficult for older women or intellectual women than it is for older or intellectual men. While this is galling, it is not part of a coherent picture of male domination and female subordination as it once was. At least now there are many women working in the media. Some are not simply successful but very powerful, such as Rosie Boycott, editor of the *Daily Express*. In some areas of the media, to be young and female is a definite advantage; in the late 1990s the fashion has been for female newsreaders. It would be wrong to suggest male domination is the most significant unfairness. Now the dominance of the media by a certain class, certain families even, and the absence of ethnic minorities are much more striking. There are now different unfairnesses coming from different places and causes. When gender is significant, it is not always women who are disadvantaged.

Some people recognize that reality has changed, that something is up. Invariably this recognition leads to questions such as 'What does it mean to be a feminist now?' or 'What can feminism tell us about this new reality?' The publishing world is full of editors hunting for the young feminist who will galvanize new audiences with a contemporary version of the old theme of female oppression. In other words, there's a search for a feminist 'take' on contemporary society. But feminism will never be relevant in that clear-sighted simple way again. Gender remains a crucial division in western society but in a much more fractured and inconsistent way. Sometimes when gender division is relevant, it is men who are disadvantaged not women.

These thoughts go into new and uncharted territory and there is not a huge amount of encouragement to undertake such a journey. Feminism is still a subject which provokes passion and, it has to be said, unreason. 'Are you for it or against it?' is the most common question. But such polarization is now unhelpful, obscuring an understanding of what feminism has achieved, what has changed, and what role gender now actually does play. It also prevents us asking an even more fundamental question: Is feminism relevant at all now?

It took me a long time before I allowed myself to ask this question. My intellectual and political formation were in feminism and it feels a bit like casting myself adrift and betraying friendships which have formed me, but for the past few years I have had a growing sense that, at some point, for my own benefit as much as anything else, I would have to look at feminism afresh, to settle my own accounts with it. I needed to understand why feminism had once been so important and why I now felt it had become a strait-jacket.

This was no overnight revelation but a growing sense of unease. Over the years I have regularly had phone calls from newspapers or magazines, or received letters from research students, asking me one or all of the following questions: Do you think feminism has achieved its goals? Would you still call yourself a feminist? Is feminism dead? I used to answer these questions reasonably confidently. Women still have a very long way to go before they reach real equality so, yes, they still need a political perspective which attends to women's specific needs. Yes, I'm still a feminist. No, feminism is not dead.

Over the last few years, though, my answers have become more and more convoluted and hesitant. I found it increasingly difficult to say I was a feminist. This was not because it was unfashionable to do so, although it was; rather it was because, almost without noticing, I had become disenchanted with the

3

idea of being 'a feminist' in such times. I still identified with the feminist objectives of abolishing discrimination based on gender and the move towards a sexually equitable society. I still cared about many of the injustices feminism cared about. But somewhere along the line, my relationship with feminism had come unstuck.

Of course, few feminists, including myself, had ever really seen themselves as fully signed up, uncritical members of some united feminist movement. Feminism wasn't like that anyway. It was more a loose alliance of women with different approaches to problems affecting women and a number of different primary concerns. So there had always been a place for ideas to be discussed critically and I had always seen myself as being on a critical wing of this broad church. The religious imagery is not accidental, however; feminism was a broad church and 'belief' is an apposite term for its dynamism. When I first encountered feminism in the 1970s, it had the force and attraction of a profound explanatory system. As the old traditional family crumbled and women began to feel the effects of post-war education and consumerism, feminism was the ideology which galvanized women, putting them in the driving seat of these profound social changes.

Certainly feminism made sense of my own experience, emerging as I did, highly educated, from university in the 1970s, yet facing ancient prejudices and discrimination. And having espoused this doctrine, it was exhilarating to be involved in the astonishing changes it made to relationships between the sexes, transforming cultural prejudices against women, knocking on the doors of workplaces and educational institutions to transform women's opportunities probably for ever.

Because of the importance which feminism had both personally and socially, it took me a long time to recognize just how uncomfortable I had become with that association. By the late 1980s, although publicly still very much associated with feminism, I was also beginning to feel compromised, drawn into interpretations of the world which no longer rang true. Throughout the 1990s I gradually realized I was travelling beyond some invisible boundary. One incident which brought this home to me was the reception given to Katie Roiphe's book, *The Morning After*, published in Britain in 1993. In reviews and features it was explained that Katie Roiphe was a young American, the daughter of a woman who had been politically active as a feminist in the 1960s and '70s. Roiphe, it was explained, had written a naïve book, the result of discovering as a student at Princeton University that the feminism which she had imbibed with her mother's milk had turned into the sour doctrine of sexual repression dressed up as political correctness.

I heard many conversations about Roiphe's book. Most were indignant in tone; what were we doing importing a book by a young American student about American sexual attitudes which were so different from our own? Why should we be worried about feminist political correctness in the USA when there were still so many steps towards equality for British women to take? Was the eagerness with which the British media had grasped this attack on feminism part of what many perceived as a growing backlash against feminism?

When I finally read the book it came as something of a surprise. It *was* naïve, but it was also a valid set of observations about the dangers of applying rigid feminist views to intimate human relationships where power does not obligingly belong to one group only. What is more, although it was a vignette of life on an American campus, it was not altogether distant and unrecognizable. What she had to say about the victim culture of feminism, about the problems with a positive discrimination programme, and especially about how relationships between the sexes might be viewed in a new, more egalitarian context, were certainly recognizable to me in the UK.

The reception of that book made me realize that although British feminists always insist that there is no single uniform feminism, only a disparate set of voices addressing women's issues, there are some no-go areas. Roiphe's book touched in a naïve way on precisely those areas, questioning the fundamental feminist convictions that women can never be powerful in

5

relationship to men and, conversely, that men can never occupy a position of vulnerability. Roiphe argued that on the sexually egalitarian campus, sexual relationships are not always characterized by male oppressors and female victims. So, however broad the church of feminism, it clearly had its limits and, like most other systems of belief, it responded with indignation and accusations of treachery to such challenges.

Feminism's self-image, as a beleaguered minority, does not help it to tolerate criticism. Women involved with feminism tend to feel they have never really had the chance to explain themselves or make a significant impact with their ideas, so what they really want is more support, not criticism. This is understandable. To call oneself a feminist has never been an easy choice and it has never made anyone popular. It is still hard for individual women to confront the injustices and plain bad behaviour that they meet in life, and to try to do something about them. More often than not, the result is marginalization, designation as a 'trouble-maker' and much *ad feminam* hostility.

Those women who fought the original battles suffer more than most. Hated and opposed when originally pushing down the barriers, they now often have to face contempt from a society which takes for granted their achievements. At a recent party I witnessed one such woman being challenged by a young man who had no sense of feminism's history or her involvement in it. 'Do you really call yourself a feminist?' he asked belligerently. 'Yes,' she answered rather wistfully, 'I'd still call myself that.' 'But what on earth does it mean?' he continued. 'I mean, is there really any need for it? Isn't it just part of the way we are, part of our unconscious?'

It was a difficult and poignant moment for me, because it encapsulated both sides of my relationship with feminism. I greatly respected the woman for what she had achieved and deplored the man's lack of respect for why she had placed herself as she did. In such circumstances, no wonder she dug her heels in. This continuing lack of credibility and acceptance explains why feminists react badly when the fundamental tenets of the movement are challenged. But when I began to examine feminist ideas critically and challenge the idea that nothing had changed, I too met with resistance. There is a real reluctance to submit feminism's fundamental assumptions to an audit to see just how relevant they are to changing realities.

The problem is that, by and large, I also agreed with what the man at that party said. Somewhere along the line something remarkable has happened. Individual feminists still meet with resistance and problems, but feminism as a movement has been extraordinarily successful; it has sunk into our unconscious. Our contemporary social world – and the way the sexes interact in it – is radically different from the one in which modern feminism emerged. Many of feminism's original objectives have been met, including the principle of equal pay for equal work, and the possibility of financial independence. Girls now are growing up in a world radically different from the one described by the early feminists. Feminism no longer has to be reiterated but simply breathed.

Few, surely, can fail to recognize that the opportunities and expectations facing young women in the new millennium make thirty years ago seem like another planet. When I left university, the sex discrimination act and equal opportunities legislation had only just become law; battles about combining careers and motherhood still lay ahead. Now, rather than feeling there are uncharted waters in front of them, young women are more likely to feel daunted by the potency of the female icons before them. In the 1980s, Margaret Thatcher destroyed the notion that women could not reach the top. And in the 1990s, stockbroker Nicola Horlick, a mother of five with a million-pound-a-year job, put paid to the idea of motherhood as an obstacle. Both women are problematic figures, certainly, and both can be called exceptions, but in the 1960s, such figures were simply unthinkable.

Feminism has, to a considerable degree, got what it wanted and most of it came to fruition in the 1980s. Jobs opened up to women; career expectations went up dramatically; most women, including many mothers, worked. Legal changes and changes in family patterns also made it possible for women to survive financially on their own should they so wish. The old morality which had restrained and oppressed women lifted. We always complain about the cliché of calling the 1980s the 'women's decade', but it was true. Rarely a month went by without another first for women, as barrier after barrier came down. The public perception of women through the '80s was that they were on a roller-coaster. The decade had begun with Margaret Thatcher becoming the first British woman prime minister, creating the strong impression that there were no longer any barriers between a very determined woman and the fulfilment of her ambitions. With the media also taking up the cause of the working mother and focusing attention on high-achieving women, it was hard not to notice women's potency.

In fact, many of the things feminism had wanted came about because of other social changes and not quite in the form anticipated. The increase in part-time and flexible working came as the result of brutal economic changes and not, as many feminists had envisaged, through a benevolent process of social relaxation. The economy was demanding the kinds of work that women could provide. At a social level, however, feminism appeared to be making little headway. The 1980s' economic boom had disguised major economic shifts and the public face of that boom was the young male 'yuppy', apparently embodying male economic power. Combined with Margaret Thatcher's overt hostility to feminism and her lack of support for women in general, it is easy to see now why so many feminists imagined that nothing was changing.

At the same time, it took a peculiar form of blindness to ignore the profound changes which were affecting men in the same period. In the 1970s the problem confronting women was how to reverse the dip in achievement and expectation which seemed to afflict teenage girls prior to their disappearing off the career ladder altogether. From the end of the 1980s, the main worry over teenagers became the poor performance of boys, not of girls. While the morale of girls and women is high, and expectations about future careers robust, the opposite appears to be true of boys. Throughout the 1990s, boys' performance at school took a nosedive.

This was just a symptom of a wider shift, of the fact that the changes affecting women's position have intersected with very great changes for men in their working patterns, in their family roles and in their social expectations. A number of forces came together at the end of the 1980s: the changes in the type of work available, a massive increase in unemployment and job insecurity which affected men very badly, and a growing pinpointing of crime and social disaffection as a male problem.

From the end of the 1980s onwards, it was men in the eye of the storm not women. First came evidence that the job market was beginning to discriminate against men. More men than women were losing their jobs and 'male' industries were closing down while areas of women's work were expanding. The new patterns of work – part-time and flexible – seemed geared to women not men. There was also evidence that men were finding the changes more difficult than women; some perceived the shifts in the family as entirely to their disadvantage, and were, in some communities, seriously disaffected.

The social and economic policies of the 1980s created extraordinary changes in the relative position of the sexes, but they also created enormous divisions between groups that went far beyond discrimination based on sex. Social disaffection, poverty and crime were visible and unsettling; there was talk of an underclass. A series of horrendous crimes fed anxieties that society was in some way falling apart. Social commentators and politicians began to question the liberalization of society which had so changed family morality. Feminism was heavily implicated in their scenarios of doom.

As a journalist writing throughout this period, it was impossible not to notice what was happening. If women had been the leading political subjects of the 1970s, men became the political problem of the 1990s. Subtly, men and their dilemmas had moved centre-stage; no longer willingly standing aside while women took priority but increasingly expressing concern at having been moved aside. The changes affecting men and the changes men themselves were making now occupied the centre of attention in a strange echo of what had happened to women twenty years previously. Whatever you made of it, there was no way this was the same society as that originally described by feminism. These changes made feminism's theoretical assumptions seem questionable, its political aims problematic and its expectation that men should cheer at the sidelines while women ran the race to the top, naïve.

Nor were men so willing to accept feminism's version of themselves; the days of genial masochism were over. In the 1970s they might have shared a sense of themselves as consistently advantaged over women. Now many were questioning this, alongside a growing belief that women have wrested power and advantages from those who are already diminished. As this new mood began to surface, feminism could have re-evaluated its previous assumptions. Instead, it tried to fit the changing landscape into the old models, ridiculing the idea of a male crisis, and taking men's complaints as further proof of their intransigence. What else would you expect from threatened potentates? This was typical of feminism's reluctance to let go of certain fundamental tenets: the insistence on the primacy of gender, a reluctance to rethink power relations, a refusal to abandon those old assumptions about oppression.

Only one writer came up with a viable idea to deal with this new male mood, but what a useful idea it was! 'Backlash', a term taken from the title of Susan Faludi's book (1991), threw feminism a lifeline just when it might have sunk. In many ways, *Backlash*, the book, is impressive. It has a firm grasp of the social and economic movements of the 1980s. Faludi looks both at the cultural representations of women, in newspaper articles, films, sitcoms and so on, as well as at the minutiae of women's earnings and women's political activities. Setting the two against each other, she concludes that women's political and economic progress was paralleled by a series of growing preoccupations which operated to undermine women's progress – stereotypes such as the childless career woman who is not only a tragic figure but also potentially a mad and dangerous one, as portrayed by Glenn Close in the film *Fatal Attraction* (1987).

When Faludi interpreted expressions of hostility to feminism in terms of a backlash against women's achievements, however she handed feminism a most impressive weapon against accepting that society had really changed. From her perspective, it was possible to interpret any number of phenomena, from films to newspaper concerns with career women, to hesitancy over positive discrimination programmes, as manifestations of a deeper underlying principle: male resistance to female progress. With a concept like this to play with, the idea that a new order might emerge from women's changing status interacting with rapid changes in men's lives was simply ruled out of court. What remained intact was the idea of men's structural power over women which they would fight to hold on to at all costs. For many feminists, the idea that all men have power over all women remains fundamental, in spite of male protests to the contrary. From this perspective, the proposition that men might be experiencing some kind of crisis of their own is just part of an attempt to derail the needs of the truly powerless group.

Here I could see I was seriously travelling in a different direction. Many women fell on the idea of backlash as the new feminism, whereas I disliked its assumption that men would inevitably seek to oppose and challenge women's equality. But I wasn't surprised that the idea was so popular. Such assumptions were everywhere, especially in what I have called 'womanism', a sort of popularized version of feminism which acclaims everything women do and disparages men. Womanism is feminism's vulgate. It asserts that women are the oppressed or the victims and never the collaborators in the 'bad' things that men do. It entails a double standard around sexuality where women's sexual self-expression is seen as necessary and even desirable, but men's is seen as dangerous or even disgusting. Womanism is by no means confined to a tiny, politically motivated bunch of man-hating feminists, but is a regular feature of mainstream culture. It fuels the tabloids and the broadsheets alike. Womanism is a convenient response to many of the uglier aspects of the great convulsions shaking modern society; the very convulsions that are, in other aspects, delivering what feminism demanded.

Of course, many men, especially social commentators, have not responded any better. They have indulged in nostalgia and made various attempts to push the genie back into the bottle. They made it easy for feminism to justify ignoring the changes. But both sides seemed to me to be insisting that there was only one relevant question for understanding sexual relationships: given the gender divide, which sex has power?

I knew that I had finally crossed some invisible boundary when, after New Labour came to power in May 1997, I began to feel so ambivalent about the activities of feminists at the highest level of government. The establishment of a women's unit and the appointment of a women's ministry did not fill me with joy and enthusiasm, nor did the sight of 'Blair's Babes', the huge increase in the number of female MPs ensured by the policy of all-women shortlists. Of course I was pleased to see all those women at last changing the appearance of the Houses of Parliament and promising to change the culture too. I ought to have been delighted to see people with the same history as myself now able to argue the feminist corner, fighting for greater equality between the sexes of all levels of society. So why feel uneasy?

This was not the usual radical unease – that feminists in government are prepared to do too little, are too cautious, too ready to kowtow to the limitations imposed by a government determined to carry majority consent with it at all times; instead, it was caused by the conflict between the certainties of this new feminist regime and my own perception that there were real social changes underway no longer easily understood by these feminist ideas. I thought we needed to look at what was happening to the sexes, without the preconceptions that one group still has power and the other needs special privileges to compensate for this. Yet here was a women's unit confidently telling us it would champion 'women's interests', apparently taking it for granted that we all knew what these were, so that we would finally be on the way to that elusive equality. The unit took for granted as truth that very rhetoric which I was beginning to question.

While these tendencies were steadily building a power base, I had been travelling in the opposite direction. I'd let go of the fundamental proposition that women are by definition oppressed. I began to wonder what it means to have institutions fighting for 'women's interests' at the beginning of the new millennium. But no discussion was forthcoming. Everyone seemed to know what women's interests were, from types of childcare, through assumptions about what women want and what men are, to the continued need for privileging women in order to further their equality. In contrast, I wanted a more honest appraisal about whether women are consistently discriminated against and what different women really want now in terms of work, childcare and mothering.

Once you let go of feminism's fundamental propositions, the world looks very different. In the West in the 1990s the meaning of gender has changed and so too has its significance in relation to other aspects of society. Interpreting these changes from the perspective of an unchanging model of male power seemed to be less and less tenable. Instead I could see situations where men were really becoming vulnerable and women potent. And I was worried that because it did not share this realization, feminism could end up allying itself with socially divisive and bigoted ideologies which attack and blame poor men for all society's problems.

So this is the complex context of men's and women's relationships as we enter the new millennium. Many aspects of the feminist vision are within grasp but not in the form originally envisaged. Instead of the rout of men sought by the radical feminists or the cosy co-operation envisaged by the socialist feminists, the 90s has been a sexually uncomfortable and sometimes antagonistic time. Oliver James, the psychiatrist, has described it as a time of 'gender rancour'. There is much confusion about how to interpret this antagonism and neither sex has covered itself in glory when trying to do so. Some women have fallen back on old simplicities about men's power and women's moral superiorities. Some men have called for traditional solutions so that they can feel comfortable again.

This book is a detailed account of what has been happening between the sexes. What is the truth about the so-called male crisis? Is it an illusion? Or has men's position really changed for the worse? If so, is this descent of man anything to do with the ascent of woman? What has been feminism's contribution to these complex economic changes? Has it been useful in keeping gender in mind or has it simply hung on to its old ideologies and policies, involving a problematic blindness to the most vulnerable groups of men? And if blind to the different degrees of vulnerability of men, is it possible that feminism might have helped demonize certain groups, disguising rather than illuminating what is really happening in society.

This book has three key themes: families and parenting; the increasingly problematic socialization of boys and young men; and the fraught area of sexual relations. In each it is clear that feminism clings to the fundamental tenet that women are by definition the oppressed party. In each case this obscures what is really happening and can produce public reactions and social policies which can be retrograde and divisive. And in each case, by clinging to its old tenets, feminism fails to see that it has been successful, that it has changed society in deep and unforeseen ways. It is time that feminism faced up to the problems of its success.

So first I examine where feminism came from, why it was necessary in the 1970s and the ideas that drove it on (Chapter 1). In Chapter 2 I look at the tidal wave of social emancipation that resulted and how feminism's fundamental ideas spread into the area of personal interaction where perhaps they were not as illuminating as they had been in the public areas of work, leisure and politics. Feminism's demand for women's rights began to become problematic and Chapter 3 looks at the success feminism had despite, rather than because of, its best intentions. The whirlwind of economic change in the 1980s, which bears the name of a woman, 'Thatcherism', delivered women the economic role that feminism demanded but without the accompanying social benefits and at the direct cost of many men. Families and communities were torn apart and by the 1990s men had become a problem.

In Chapter 4, I look at this unexpected turn in sexual relations and how feminism's response was to deny rather than face up to the crisis of masculinity, to the fact that men were being forced to change by economic realities. This was a missed opportunity; hadn't feminism demanded that traditional male values and behaviour should change? But it was hostile economic forces, not feminism, which brought this about. So when (Chapter 5) men appeared vulnerable, with a significant increase in the suicide rate, feminism had no help to offer. In fact, men were losing moral authority in the family and on the public stage, a change which should have had an entirely positive effect on the balance of power between the genders (Chapters 6 and 7). Unfortunately, the centre of moral certainty was gravitating towards women (Chapter 8), not just swinging against men. It produced a situation where on the one hand some men identified with the self-mockery of Nick Hornby and *Men Behaving Badly*, and, on the other, women adopted the posture of superwoman, and no one quite believed the rhetoric.

Women were unsure of what it all meant and many found it easier to take refuge in 'womanism' than to take seriously a growing crisis of masculinity (Chapter 9), so it is not surprising that womanism gave birth to a reaction, a call for the need to reassert traditional masculine values and male authority (Chapter 10). This confrontation of views, of reasserting the traditional emotional divisions between the sexes, however, was and is profoundly out of touch with how parenting is being done, with the choices both sexes are making, with the way in which young males are being socially stigmatized and in the conduct of sexuality. These simplifications about gender have turned out to be worse than useless in explaining what is really going on. In fact, they have been actively misleading, disguising other problems which needed to be recognized. So the final chapters of this book are devoted to examining each of these in turn. I look at how social problems involving young men and boys are not caused by gender in a simple way but because they are at the sharp end of dramatic changes in the mix of our society (Chapters 11 and 14). Around parenting too (Chapters 12 and 13), gender simplifications have muddied our perceptions, preventing us from recognizing how people are living their lives and what really concerns them. Finally I look at how gender relations are in fact much more complex and muddled. When it comes to some of the controversial sexual issues of the times – sexual harassment (Chapter 15) and date rape (Chapter 16) – the old polarities of men as powerful oppressors and women as passive victims simply will no longer work.

In short, feminism has succeeded beyond the wildest dreams of the brave women who fought its first battles. Its future in the new millennium is to face up to the problems of its success, and to see gender as just one possible reason for social and personal conflicts rather than an all-encompassing cause. But if it is going to be capable of making these changes, it will first have to let go of its sacred cows.

1 THE ASSAULT ON UNEARNED MALE POWER

Think-tanks and universities regularly commission research on young women's attitudes to feminism. Why, they ask, do young women no longer respond to the clarion call of feminism? Meanwhile, publishers are puzzled because they cannot anywhere find a new young feminist who will set hearts racing. Perhaps, they speculate, contemporary writers lack the flair of earlier feminists. Or perhaps young women themselves are more selfish and fainthearted. Perhaps it's 'the backlash'. Whatever the reason, the effect is clear; whoever and however they try, the fundamental idea of women's oppression fails to inspire contemporary young women.

All I can say is that it was not ever thus. When I encountered feminism in the 1970s, it was quite simply electrifying. I recognized immediately that notions of male power and oppression had direct relevance for my own life. Feminism illuminated frustrations I had met and offered a way out. And this was in the face of considerable media and family hostility to such views. In the early 1970s, feminism was just as unpopular as it is said to be now by the backlash theorists. Then it was tarnished with the image of the Miss World protests; feminists were seen as a bunch of sexually promiscuous bra-burners. Anyone taking up the cause knew that at some point they would be accused of hating children, families and men. My father certainly – as part of a series of more complicated views – warned me that fighting for sexual and economic autonomy would destroy men's respect for me.

Such opposition, however, simply could not override my conviction that feminism was relevant and made sense to me. The calls for equality of opportunity, for greater personal fulfilment, for an end to women basing their lives on childcare and domestic subservience, and the challenge to the automatic superiority assumed by men, echoed my own experiences. Feminism also seemed to offer a model for new and better relationships with men. For those of us who took it on board, it resonated at an emotional level.

It is not hard to see why. Arriving at university in the 1970s it was almost inevitable that any woman with ambitions and a critical stance on society would be drawn to this dynamic new ideology. It was in and around higher education that feminism found its most fertile ground. Most of the women who threw themselves into feminist politics in Britain came from among the well-educated. We got to university after schooling which had subtly directed girls away from 'male' subjects, steering them instead towards 'female' subjects with lower career expectations. Ahead lay the overt discrimination of the job market which at the time was assumed to be the natural order of things.

When I started at Cambridge University only three out of the twenty-odd colleges, were for women. Men outnumbered women by eight to one. There was still an overt culture of misogyny: there were men's clubs, men-only sports with their attendant prestigious culture, men-only dining clubs. The academic staff were dominated by men; female professors were still eccentric oddities. Admittedly, Cambridge was 'old establishment' but it also mirrored pretty exactly the establishment which ruled Britain. It was easy to see in microcosm the exclusion of women from wider positions of political, social and economic power.

Women often did extremely well academically but even so it was no passport to equal employment. Certain kinds of employment were still closed to women. Even though I entered the job market after the introduction of equal opportunities and sex discrimination legislation in the mid-1970s, there had been few changes in traditional working patterns. Many jobs were still considered 'men's' or 'women's' jobs and there were significant disparities of earnings as a consequence. Jobs which we now take for granted as being open to both sexes – stockbroking, some sections of the media, engineering, architecture, medicine and so on – were then totally male dominated. Because women and men continued to be employed in sex-segregated areas, there were few opportunities to challenge unequal earnings directly.

When I became aware of feminism, the situation was not hugely different from that described by Betty Friedan in her milestone work, *The Feminine Mystique* (1963). She wrote of the 'female malaise' of many university-educated women who did not use their education but were condemned to lives of stultifying boredom as housewives. In the 1970s women already made up 35 per cent of the workforce and most graduates certainly expected to work. Yet most employers still assumed that women would eventually give up careers in favour of families. As a result, prejudice against women employees was still widespread.

The job market was shaped by the assumption that women would ultimately drop out of work. Job interviews routinely included questions to women about their marriage and child-bearing plans. In one job interview my male rival was asked what his career plans were for the next ten years, a question which gave him the opportunity to shine. I was asked a series of (now illegal) questions about my hopes for a family and how that affected my career expectations. They were questions designed to put my commitment to the job (or lack of it) on trial.

Such assumptions lay behind the discriminatory practices in employment at that time. Employers justified excluding women because they would soon be claimed by families. Women scaled down their own ambitions for similar reasons. Childcare was almost non-existent, so the idea that a career and motherhood were, if not totally incompatible, then at least extremely difficult to combine, was accurate. When women thought about careers, they imagined difficult choices, between career and children, or at least between uninterrupted career and children.

At the time feminists fighting for equality often felt the struggle was a lonely and groundbreaking one. With the benefit of hindsight, it now looks as if feminism was the only logical way out of the bottleneck caused by the convergence of a number of social changes. However much the immediate post-war era had been a time of homecoming and home-making, the Second World War had opened new horizons for women; they had occupied all sorts of 'unfeminine' roles and professions while the men were away. Afterwards, individual women made gradual breakthroughs into various spheres of work. This legacy was inherited by the generation of well-educated women who emerged in the 1960s and 1970s, thanks to the equal educational opportunities given to girls in the post-war years. Demands for equal opportunities outside education as well were inevitable.

There were also more jobs, and more of them suitable for women. The main expansion of the labour market had been in the service sectors, opening up jobs in leisure, tourism, retail, design, information and catering; old-fashioned sexism was not so relevant here. Yet at the same time, all the old assumptions about motherhood as the great hiatus in women's lives still dominated employment practices. Together with the general push throughout the 1960s to increase equality and human rights, these contradictory forces created a bottleneck, out of which feminism emerged.

This is not to say that social changes would have happened without feminism. In the 1990s several expanding Asian economies have drawn on female labour without any emancipation of women. Feminism in the West was a progressive, modernizing politics with a strong belief in equal rights and justice. It attracted women with an interest in wider political justice and it had to fight against a powerful element which strongly opposed any change in the traditional family structure. This is why, even at the time, it was not a mass movement, rather it belonged to a potent minority.

Those who did devote their time and energies to challenging the old assumptions were drawn by an 'emotional agenda' which several feminists recognize now as being the resolute determination not to live like their own mothers. 'We would be different from our own mothers,' Angela Phillips has said recently. 'We were going out to work and our partners would share the childcare with us' (*Guardian*, 20 January 1998). The mothers of feminists were the women who, in the relief of the war's aftermath, gave up most of their own ambitions in order to build a better future for their children. Many transferred those frustrated ambitions to their daughters. Latterly, in more reflective mode, almost all the active feminists of the 1960s and '70s remember having heard their mothers describe how they had 'given up everything' for their families and warning their daughters not to make the same mistakes. To the liberated spirits of the 1960s and '70s, the defeated hopes and ambitions of wives and mothers, their dependency on men, their submersion in the family, all looked like suffering on a grand scale. Feminism made sense to women because it offered a way out.

Feminism was never only about jobs. Demands for equal pay and sex discrimination legislation were accompanied by demands to end 'legal and financial discrimination' as well as a more general and diffuse attack on all social activities which gave men privileges and discriminated against or belittled women. These included demands for 'the right to control your own fertility' and for 'self-determined' sexuality. Alongside that lay even more nebulous calls for sexual freedom, 'autonomy' and 'self-fulfilment'.

In most feminists' minds, these more diffuse aspects of social discrimination were closely connected with economic discrimination. They saw that many of the legal and financial structures affecting women, as well as attitudes towards appropriate family and sexual behaviour, reflected the economic model of father as breadwinner and provider for a dependent woman. In the 1970s welfare, taxation and provision of benefits still all assumed a household of a breadwinning father with financial dependants – women and children. Men could claim a married person's tax allowance. Since the primary role for the woman was in the home, any income she had was treated as joint income. Married couples were taxed jointly, the taxation deducted from the husband's pay. Benefits were paid to households on the assumption that men alone provided the family income. One example was supplementary benefit for a dependent spouse and children in the case of sickness. This was paid only to a man; a woman was not entitled to claim even if she was the main earner in the family. Feminists claimed these structures had been built on the model of the patriarchal family which had dominated English society for centuries and in which men exercised almost total control over their wives' property and persons.

Fighting the discrimination – legal, political, sexual and emotional too – based on this patriarchal model was at the heart of modern feminism. Indeed, the infantilizing of women by the father-dominated family was feminism's 'big idea'. Women wanted the right to be autonomous, to support themselves by earning their own living. This was as much an ethical as an economic position. It was quite simply wrong for tax and benefits to assume women's dependency on men; such assumptions discriminated against those who wanted to be or had to be financially independent. Worse, an acceptance of this model meant a tacit acceptance that men were superior.

Logically, most people with a broadly egalitarian and democratic view of society, even those unsympathetic to feminists' lifestyles, could see the justice of this criticism of patriarchal social structures. So, intellectually and morally, feminism carried the day. Social and economic discrimination was easy to prove. Nor was it difficult to highlight the drudgery and hardship typical of the lives of women who were stuck at home or those who remained responsible for the home even when working. Even the routine belittling of women in images was acknowledged as supporting male privilege and discrimination against women.

Feminist objections to this notion of male power also went much further, extending into a critique of the sexual and emotional structures of society. These touched on much more problematic areas: lifestyle and sexual choices. It is this aspect of feminism – overthrowing traditional sexual and behavioural restraints – that tends to be remembered. What comes to mind rather than economic and legal reforms are the pro-abortion marches, the protests against the Miss World beauty contest, the changed sexual self-presentation of women, Germaine Greer posing naked for a Dutch porn magazine.

Perhaps this is not wholly surprising. After all, the violent upheavals of the 1960s which transformed the face of British society for good were to do with radical changes in sexual behaviour and lifestyle. In some ways feminism was just part and parcel of a profound revolution in which the old values of sexual repression, monogamy, life-long commitment, paternalistic family responsibility (and the hypocrisy which sometimes went with that) came under attack; The arrival of a safe contraceptive in the form of the pill made this possible. When social commentators rue the '60s as the era which gave birth to the 'me generation' whose pursuit of individual gratification destroyed the old altruistic bonds of community and family, they invariably include feminism in this.

As it happens, feminism was as much challenge to this ethos as part of it. The political and sexual libertarians of the time, embodied in magazines like *Oz*, were challenging the old structures, the old restrictions, and the old hypocrisies which stunted them emotionally and sexually. Early feminists, however, spotted a 'double oppression' of women in this libertarian talk. Sheila Rowbotham has described how, working for the radical magazine *Black Dwarf* in the '60s, she became disillusioned with its contemptuous attitude to women, 'chicks' as they were called in these circles. Women like her realized that if traditional society had sexually repressed respectable women while exploiting the so-called disreputable women, the libertarian agenda wasn't much better. Even anti-establishment radicals were capable of extreme contempt for women, as the American black activist, Eldridge Cleaver, summed up when he made his unforgettable comment: 'Women's position in the revolution is prone.'

Without the sexual revolution there would have been no feminism. But feminism also upped the ante. What was essentially a generation freeing itself up to enjoy a consumer society based on extreme individualism, became in feminist hands a tougher and more difficult fight about equal rights and equal treatment. Feminism had focused on a deeper problem, of discrimination based on gender so that masculinity conferred advantages and femininity guaranteed disadvantages. Power was no longer being seen in exclusively political terms; it was also seen to operate in less obvious ways – through sexual assumptions, sexual behaviour and attitudes.

Everything changed so rapidly in the wake of feminism that it is easy to forget what society was like before. Indeed, when Melanie Phillips writes that contemporary family problems are caused by 'the loss of male authority' (*Times Literary Supplement*, 20 March 1998), one wonders if she has forgotten the suffering caused by the imposition of patriarchy. Maybe it is easy to forget. There is a huge gulf between the kinds of sexual and familial decisions which women were forced to take before and after this social upheaval. The Profumo affair which so scandalized British society in the early '60s seems to belong not just to earlier decades but an earlier century. Then it was utterly scandalous and dangerous for an establishment figure to be seen to mix with women whose sexual morality was even faintly questionable. By today's standards what happened seems so trivial; then it was enough to bring down a government.

Even in recent years we have had poignant reminders of the restraints society once imposed on women; and of how quickly the world changed after the combined forces of 'free love' and feminism overturned the old morality. There was huge sympathy for Clare Short in 1996 when it became known that she had given away her baby for adoption in the mid-1960s, merely because she became pregnant before marrying the baby's father. It has recently been revealed that Joni Mitchell, doyenne of the sexual revolution, had a baby daughter whom she too gave up for adoption. Even in the early 1960s, for a respectable girl to have a child out of marriage was a source of deep shame to many families.

There are many heartbreaking stories which explain exactly why women needed to overthrow hypocrisy and double standards. A few years ago I interviewed a woman in her eighties in connection with a television series, *The Hidden History of Sex*. When not quite twenty, she had become pregnant on a first date after being virtually raped. She did not fully understand what was happening and only realized when her mother challenged her that she was seven months pregnant. Her parents threw her out of the house; she found her way to a nursing home in London. Her parents ignored her, but a few days after the baby was born, her mother visited her and told her she would adopt the baby herself but that there was never again to be any mention of what had happened. The baby boy was then brought up as her brother. The woman later married and failed to have any more children, so she went out of her way to treat him specially but could never tell him. After she agreed to talk on the television programme when she was eighty and her son sixty, she told him. But he rebuffed her, asking why she had chosen to do this to him now.

Such tragedies show exactly why the sexual revolution was necessary. Women were being controlled by something deeper: age-old assumptions about appropriate lifestyles and behaviours and a contempt for women who strayed. Hence women's demands for the right to sexual self-discovery, and the right to have a sexual life without judgement. All of this entailed challenging assumptions about sex premised on male superiority: the hypocrisy which accepted men's sexual desires as normal but castigated women for theirs; women's rights to control their own fertility rather than being at the whim of men's desires (with consequent unwanted pregnancy); the taking of the male body as norm with the consequence that female health and sexual problems were regarded with a combination of neglect and disgust.

Although all these looked like exclusively sexual issues, in feminists' minds they were intertwined and based on models of male power and female dependency. Much of the passion invested in the pursuit of sexual liberation came from the belief that challenging sexual stereotypes and pursuing personal fulfilment necessarily also spelled the end of a society based on

25

the hierarchical father-dominated family and related notions of male supremacy. Feminism viewed this as a struggle against an old and tenacious social form; history showed that under the patriarchal model, in law, if not always in practice, women were little more than sexual chattel. Until reforms in the nineteenth century, a wife could be divorced at the man's will, if a woman was unfaithful she lost all rights, fathers had automatic rights over children, fathers could marry off their daughters. In short, a woman's sexuality, body and reproduction were very much controlled by husbands and fathers.

So these challenges to sexual attitudes were also challenges to the unearned power and authority of the father with its culture of dependency, emotional infantilism and misogyny. And what had until that point been taken for granted as the 'feminine' way to live – a journey from obedient girl to subservient wife and devoted mother – was now described as sexist, the cultural expression of the control and dominance implicit in the patriarchal family. When feminism attacked 'patriarchy', it was attacking the whole package of men's power – economic, legal, sexual and emotional. Even though Ibsen's vision of the *Doll's House* had been written a hundred years previously, most feminists thought it still pretty well summed up the inevitable female subordination in the patriarchal family. This is why feminists were invariably hostile to the traditional family.

Perhaps given the state of society at the time, it is not surprising that feminism's rhetoric was borrowed from ideas of freedom fighting and a struggle against a powerful oppressor. The parallel was appropriate but also questionable. Feminist demands and visions were couched in terms like female autonomy, women's freedom, women's rights, women's self-determination. It was the language of anti-imperialist struggles, the right of colonized nations and people to define their own objectives, to win full political and economic subjectivity and to define their own status. This imagery and much of feminism's impetus, came from the American civil rights movement.

The imagery also had a metaphorical richness. Women could see a parallel between their lives and those of slaves and colonized peoples. They felt defined as second-class citizens and restricted by their gender from having the same expectations as the other half of the population. They talked of women's 'colonized' bodies, their fertility and sexuality controlled by what men wanted, not by themselves. With that rhetoric went assumptions about male power. If women were deprived of equal rights by virtue of their gender, it followed that men had corresponding advantages. Men were potent oppressors and, however diminished their own particular circumstances, they would also have this familial power over women. Consequently, women must constitute a class or caste of people whose identities and experiences as women were much more important than any other social factors.

Male power meant different things to different feminists. Few went so far as radical feminist Sheila Jeffries who, at one conference I attended, described men as 'phallic imperialists'. That idea implied not just that the male gender conferred power, but that men actively went out to subjugate and dominate women simply by virtue of their gender. Historian Barbara Taylor also points out that 'the notion of women as powerless victims of male power never went entirely uncriticized'. Socialist feminists always believed 'that male power over women was in a sense a derivative secondary form of power, essentially derived from who had control over the economy'. But she acknowledges an elementary consensus about male power and the moral superiority conferred on men by virtue of their gender. 'We called that "the patriarchy", the favourite term for that organized male power over men as we imagined it to be' (interview with author).

Even at the time some feminists doubted just how appropriate this language was for relationships between men and women. The father clearly had authority and power, but was the model of colonization, implying capture and defeat of one type of society by another, followed by domination and slavery, really appropriate as a metaphor for the more complex bond of a sexual relationship? After all, women were not captured and enslaved against their will, even if they were curtailed by financial dependency. Indeed, many social historians have insisted that the twentieth century, unlike previous periods, is characterized by affectionate, companionate marriage rather than coercion.

Marriage could also entail advantages for women. If a woman was married to a rich man, could we really think of her as a member of an oppressed group? She might have the misfortune to be married to a violent bully or her husband might divorce her and leave her penniless. Indeed, even thirty years later, the whole sorry scenario which unfolded around Princess Diana and her marginalization by a powerful family was a reminder that even the most glamorous and apparently powerful women can suffer in a rigidly patriarchal family. In such cases, even the richest woman might experience the types of discrimination which could and did afflict women.

Then again, she might not. Instead she might remain comfortably married, and even if not 'fulfilled', she might partake of all the privileges and power which accrued to a powerful husband. Unless it is assumed that all men bully, exploit and control their wives, leave them as soon as their breasts sag, beat them for pleasure, rape them, stop them from experiencing any kind of personal development, then it is impossible to assume women never share in the privileges of their husbands or never, in emotional terms, have power within households.

There were other disconcerting elements in this rhetoric too. Somewhere lodged in it was an agenda for the emotions; 'autonomy' was seen as crucial not just economically but emotionally too and that gave work almost moral status as the principal means to this autonomy. An ambiguity towards children followed from this. Feminists, being women, were obviously concerned with acknowledging the overwhelming importance which children had in women's lives. But in equal measures they regarded them as 'a problem' or 'a threat' to that financial autonomy. Behind all these calls for autonomy, self-determination, self-fulfilment, there was a rejection not just of the actual social and political models of male dominance, but also a rejection of a model of emotional dependency which was assumed to come with it; dependency is infantilism, commitment is imprisonment, loyalty is possession.

There were many bizarre manifestations of this, such as 'the politics of anti-monogamy' which elevated casual sex into an act of political liberation. I'm not sure how much people were deliberately deluding themselves in order to have a good time, but they certainly put on a good show of thinking that their own anti-monogamy stance would have repercussions at the political and social level. Anyone whose lifestyle seemed to break the bonds of mutual dependency and inter-relationships with men could find herself depicted as a paragon of feminist living. This included lesbianism, which some feminists represented as the ultimate freedom from men. Even with the fervour gone, along with the illusion of changing the world by sleeping with most of it, feminism is still equated in some minds with sexual independence.

In the 1970s none of this seemed odd to the people involved. These were experiments to find a way of life in which the unearned power of men could never again limit and control women's potential. But what happened as society began to change and feminism, once the discourse of the powerless, became the most potent source of change?

2

FEMINISM: A MOVEMENT BLIND TO ITS
OWN EFFECTIVENESS

Most liberal-minded people, even if they disliked what they saw as feminist behaviour (usually characterized as anti-family, selfishly careerist and sometimes sexually immoral), were prepared to accept the broad ethical position that equal rights should apply to women. Consequently there was little opposition either to the Equal Opportunities or the Sex Discrimination Acts. Most people also tolerated the criticisms of men's dominance within the family and across society generally; the restrictions this placed on women's opportunities were all too obvious. As a result, throughout the 1970s, many of feminism's propositions came to be accepted as common sense.

Feminists themselves, however, are not always ready to acknowledge the huge effect they have had on society. This is partly because one of the favourite sports of certain right-wingers has been to blame feminism for all the negative changes they detect in society. Victoria Gillick, Margaret Thatcher and Charles Murray are just a few among many who, over the last two decades, have blamed the 'me-first' philosophy of the feminist generation for undermining stable family life. This is the *reductio ad absurdum* of complex social changes. Feminists, though, often respond with their own simplicities. How can you blame feminism, they reply, when feminists themselves never had power? How can feminism have been responsible for major changes when it has only ever been a handful of women working on the margins of society?

It is true that individual feminists, such as Hillary Clinton in America or Harriet Harman and Patricia Hewitt in the UK, have only recently become prominent. Prior to the leftward shift of these countries' governments, active participation in feminist politics was always a career handicap, but it is disingenuous to conclude that feminism was marginal. Feminism had an enormous impact on society, probably a greater impact than any other social or political ideology this century. On the other hand, feminists are not lying when they play down their impact; they felt marginalized because they met opposition, rarely benefited personally and when the real changes began to happen, they were not quite as anticipated.

Yet it was feminism which changed what women thought was desirable or possible for themselves. Once the equal opportunities and sex discrimination legislation was in place, making it illegal for women to be treated unfairly, the groundwork was there for radical changes in expectations. Educational opportunities, for example, had been steadily improving for girls since the war. But in the 1970s, there were dramatic changes. Feminists who promoted anti-sexism and equal opportunities in school, colleges and the workplace played a major part in broadening horizons. Once schools and universities became self-conscious about girls' career expectations, then traditional assumptions about appropriate subjects for boys and girls began to break down.

Women's actual career prospects also began to improve as a result of feminism. Changes in the job market helped quite considerably, but again it was women's changed outlook that was critical. In the 1970s, the expanding service sector looked to a previously untapped pool of labour: women. By the 1980s it would also use the last remaining reserve of labour: mothers who, crucially, 'matched' the need for part-time, contract workers. This might have happened without feminism, but women's readiness was due to a change in consciousness.

Feminism had a transformative effect on the cultural front as well. This was much more than individual feminists being influential in the media – they weren't particularly. Individuals like Germaine Greer were regularly hauled up for bear-baiting sessions with hostile opponents. An evening with Mary

Whitehouse, the prominent anti-pornography campaigner, comes to mind, for example. But apart from these one-offs, it was more a case of feminist perspectives infiltrating most subjects. For a debate on virtually any subject, liberal programme-makers went out of their way to find someone to put the case for how gender came into the issue. Often the feminist angle carried the day.

Writers and film-makers began to document women's experiences of oppression in the home, at work and in sexual relationships. All those who fought to have women's art and writing valued will remember the initial howls of outrage. When I wrote an undergraduate dissertation on women novelists in the nineteenth century, the ratifying committee disputed whether or not this was a valid subject in literature. Those who set up Virago, initially a collective operating with limited funds, remember similar scorn. Not long after, what had started on the margins of mainstream publishing became a commercial success. Virago made its name reprinting forgotten women authors, along with contemporary feminist ideas. They had found an audience hungry for accounts of women's experiences or discussions of women's concerns. The Women's Press followed suit and then more mainstream publishers.

This was not surprising. The runaway best-sellers of the decade were all women's novels. Erica Jong's *Fear of Flying* (1971), Lisa Alther's *Kinflicks* (1976) and Marilyn French's *The Women's Room* (1977), were novels which fictionalized the journey at the heart of the feminist project; from repression in the patriarchal family to sexual self-knowledge and a new female autonomy. Taking responsibility for your life, changing it, finding a new freedom – however watered down into more acceptable mainstream forms, this female journey was the project of the decade.

Academia was also shaken by feminism. Many disciplines came quickly under scrutiny for their neglect of female subjects or experiences. Some universities welcomed women's studies options into their courses, others violently opposed them. But there were plenty of academics in other conventional subjects who recognized the impact. History was transformed by the writings of women like Sheila Rowbotham who showed how women had been 'hidden from history' English literature courses recognized how their great tradition almost invariably excluded all but a handful of women writers; even science subjects had to recognize previously excluded questions of gender. As Mary Evans says in *Introducing Contemporary Feminist Thought* (1997), feminism introduced a new perspective into intellectual and academic life. This was 'the recognition that the once universal he/man of academic disciplines is only one half of the reality of human existence'.

Popular magazines like *Cosmopolitan* carried their own version of the feminist message, asserting the need for women to become more powerful in the bedroom as well as in the workplace. These magazines saw themselves as the voice of modern women, women who had a right to be equal, who were striking out for careers, who demanded a sex life to equal men's. *Cosmopolitan* may have derided dreary feminist politicos, but the main voice of modern women was feminism. It was feminism which supplied the vision of working women, and raised questions about the obstacles still in women's way. It was feminism which argued the case for overthrowing the old repressions in pursuit of greater self-knowledge and greater autonomy.

Feminists often distanced themselves from these changes when they came about in ways not quite anticipated or perhaps even not quite wanted. *Cosmopolitan* is a case in point. It shared in many of feminism's fundamental tenets, yet it carved out a version of feminism which was not always compatible with the stance of politically active feminists. *Cosmopolitan*'s version of sexual freedom and the objective of a have-it-all, do-it-all lifestyle, with its emphasis on consumerism and how to make yourself sexually desirable to men, often provoked ambivalence. Commenting on another new magazine, feminist academic Janice Winship sighed, 'What's new about pubescent girls in soft porn pics?' ('Magazines for Girls', 1987) Ultimately, though, these magazines were seen more as allies than foes, a recognition that their emphasis on liberalizing sexual attitudes and the building up of the female consumer, were closer to feminism than not.

Indeed, these rapid changes in the sexual mores which had previously controlled women's lives were probably the most significant changes of the period. In the 1970s, traditional life-styles which had been identified as controlling and limiting women's lives began to crumble. The institution of marriage took the most direct hit. It wasn't just that women were winning equal legal rights in marriage, although these had profound implications for women's status in marriage; nor was it that many women were beginning to argue that becoming a wife and mother should not spell the end of careers. Women had begun to reject the institution of marriage altogether.

Reform of the divorce law in the 1960s had made divorce easier. By the 1970s the notion of marriage as an indissoluble union had gone. Simultaneously, the new sexual freedoms, and awareness of the restrictions that traditional marriage placed on women, meant there were increasing numbers of unmarried cohabitees and children born outside marriage. The improvement in women's economic position combined with welfare provision for single parents meant that unmarried parenthood, whether through divorce or choice, became not just thinkable but common. Combined with women winning increased rights in divorce settlements, especially around economic provision, these changes amounted to very great improvements in women's legal status as sexual partners and mothers.

Once under attack, the old attitudes changed with astonishing rapidity. By the mid-1970s, attitudes towards unwanted pregnancies, to living together before marriage and even to having children outside marriage had been transformed. By the 1980s, the vast increase in cohabiting unmarried couples with and without children was *the* most significant demographic trend and the most significant source of worry to the moralists. With the exception of the two world wars, the proportion of births outside marriage had remained stable for fifty years at 4 per cent of the population. By the late 1980s, 25 per cent of all children born in England were born outside marriage.

In less than fifteen years, society had moved from viewing extra-marital sex as shameful to the abolition of all stigma for those who have children outside marriage. Indeed, in contemporary society, so total has been this change that however hard politicians try to reverse public opinion, there is no longer any real disgrace in pregnancy outside a stable relationship. In the 1990s Madonna, Michele Pfeiffer and Jodie Foster were just a few among many who had babies 'on their own', asserting their 'right' to have children. By the mid-1990s, the stigma attached to a healthy, normal-aged, single mother had disappeared so completely that the problem with this event was located in another place altogether as far as the media were concerned: people no longer worried about the morality of errant females, only whether such women had rendered men redundant altogether.

Without knowing I was part of the most significant demographic trend of this century, I did my bit for these statistics. I was able to start living with someone without having to think about taking the step of formal commitment; there was no question about not earning my own living and in so far as I thought about marriage I thought about it in negative terms as involving a loss of identity, a loss of financial autonomy, an abdication of my independence and identity to the unearned authority of someone whom I wanted to see as my equal. The question of making a formal commitment arose only when we had children. By then, however, we had been together long enough to feel that we would stay together because we wanted to and because of our commitment to the children rather than because we had been told to do so by 'patriarchal' institutions.

My motives were explicitly connected with feminist arguments, but I suspect they were typical of the millions of other women who made the same lifestyle choices at the same time without a similar involvement in feminist politics. Marriage had quite simply lost its hold and however much feminism might now want to distance itself from what is often called the disintegration of the family, it was at the emotional epicentre of these changes in family life and sexual behaviour. It was the feminist argument on behalf of autonomy, equality, and the need to be freed from the emotional and sexual infantilism of traditional marriage which underpinned and justified so many of the reforms in family law and practice and changes in behaviour.

Looking back at this period with the advantage of hindsight, the transformations were so rapid that it is hard not to imagine the door was already partly open when feminism pushed on it. 'A fair wind was blowing behind women's liberation,' one male writer has noted. 'Even conservative men couldn't stop them' (Jack O'Sullivan, in G. Dench, *Rewriting the Sexual Contract* [1998]). But to feminists active at the time, it did not feel like that. To push over the traces of the old society, to transform tradition into a desire for democratic and equal relations, to win that moral and ethical high ground, feminists were in constant argument and meeting constant opposition and hostility. I have an outlaw mother (how can you have an in-law if you are not married?) who still finds it hard to forget I am not legally married.

It is also easy to imagine that because the changes look so inevitable now, 1970s' feminists were unnecessarily po-faced and extreme about getting their ideas over. Anyone who doubts how hard that struggle was should take a look at the interviews with leading feminists in Susan Mitchell's book *Icons, Saints and Divas* (1997). The women she talked to all wrote books in the 1960s and '70s which 'changed' lives; Erica Jong's *Fear of Flying* (1971) coined the idea of the 'zipless fuck' as a symbol of women's sexual freedom; Phyllis Chessler's *Women and Madness* (1972) is the definitive study of how women's struggles against oppressive institutions were often categorized as madness; Kate Millet's *Sexual Politics* (1970) runs through English literature exposing the utterly damaging stereotypes which surrounded women; and Robin Morgan, editor of *Sisterhood is Powerful* (1970), coined the phrase 'the personal is political', also popularizing the idea of sisterhood. These are all books which exerted massive cultural influence, yet the frustrations and slights accorded to their authors show just how much hostility could be expected and how few personal rewards were on hand.

Interestingly, most of these authors reject the idea that there has been real change in women's position. Mostly they endorse Susan Faludi's theory that contemporary society is characterized by a backlash against feminist ideas. As Erica Jong puts it: 'We're a long way from having a truly equal society where both genders have equal input intellectually, financially, politically, sexually; a long, long way. Sometimes I wonder if we'll ever have it.'

This attitude is typical of what happened to feminism in the 1980s. Feminists barely acknowledged the significance of what we now know to be the momentous changes which were taking place around them and because of them. The changes were seen as either not deep enough or in danger of being over-turned. At the very moment when feminism could have changed its rhetoric as many of its objectives were being met, there was instead a reassertion of its basic propositions. Why?

Certainly one significant factor was that changes were not always easy to see, especially if you were in the thick of them and experiencing more resistance than benefit. Robin Morgan says:

> The real changes have occurred in consciousness, in lifestyle, in the labour force, in consciousness about work, in con-sciousness about violence against women, about sexuality, about recognising different kinds of families. There has been an extraordinary shift in consciousness in what is historically a very short period of time. When it's your life it seems like a damned long period of time and you think, 'Let's get on with this. I've only got one life here, I'd like to see a little progress.' (In S. Mitchell, *Icons, Saints and Divas*, 1997)

In addition, visible changes were not always easy to interpret as progressive. The increase in numbers of women working did not seem to have appreciably helped women's lot; in the 1980s feminists became much more aware of how motherhood affec-ted women's role in the economy. Statistics showed that women were simply not reaching the same levels as men, and the diffi-culties of combining childcare and work seemed almost insur-mountable. There was no real evidence that childcare would become a political priority. So, throughout the 1980s, most feminists insisted that the changes were superficial. Women, they pointed out, continued to earn on average only 75 per cent of the male salary. Career women met a 'glass ceiling' in their professions and corporate cultures. Increased career opportunities, without a redefinition of men's role in the home, looked like a double burden for women rather than a liberation.

Some of the improvements in female visibility were also double-edged. Feminists often disagreed about whether a female icon like Madonna, pushing at the boundaries of 'acceptable' sexual behaviour for women, made them more powerful or exploitable. Sexual liberation seemed to have jumped out of feminists' hands and become a much more problematic force, sometimes even producing hardcore pornography and films of grotesque violence against women. In 1984, *Dressed to Kill* coincided with the activities of the Yorkshire Ripper in the North of England, suggesting that whatever gains feminism might have been making on equal opportunities, expectations and cultural representation, misogyny was still rampant. And cultural representations aside, women's interests were still poorly represented in politics and law; women and girls still could expect hostility and even defeat when bringing charges of harassment, rape, domestic violence or child abuse. Superficially at least, not much had changed since Germaine Greer had provocatively declared that all men hate women.

Certainly, what these phenomena seemed to require was a greater depth in the understanding of both overt and covert oppression. Women were clearly constrained by more than overt discrimination; they were also constrained by deep prejudices and their own internalizing of negative attitudes. Policies to challenge these would help women achieve equality.

So although formal equality was coming within reach, there was no retreat from an analysis of male power. Rather, this was the period when it was extended into more personal areas such as domestic violence, pornography, rape and sexual harassment as work. These were all seen as areas of women's 'oppression' which had previously been invisible and had to be pulled into the light of day. Like domestic violence, they had been hidden through shame, or, like sexual harassment, rendered invisible because they were accepted as a natural part of relations between the sexes. Aspects of taken-for-granted male behaviour came under scrutiny: sexist attitudes towards women as inferior or available to be used by men; domestic violence where men felt they had a right to chastize and control their wives; rape where men sometimes claimed that they knew better than the women involved what their victims had wanted; or sexual harassment where a man might use sexualized behaviour or language to degrade or humiliate a woman. These seemed to embody the deeper obstacles to achieving total equality, rooted in assumptions about masculinity and femininity.

This was not inventing problems where there were none. Women were drawn to feminism not only because of issues like pay differentials but also because it made sense of bad experiences in their personal lives where they had been restricted, belittled or even brutalized by traditional assumptions about masculine behaviour. Feminism insisted that the analysis of male power, originally mobilized to tackle overt discrimination at work and in the family, was relevant to these deeper areas; these activities expressed the contempt and hostility which was directed towards women because of their inferior status. Power, they said, was working at the points of most intimate connection between the sexes, and in the 1980s most feminists agreed.

Natasha Walter in her book *The New Feminism* (1998) suggests that present-day feminism should ignore this former preoccupation with challenging masculine and feminine stereotypes and concentrate instead on the 'material inequalities'. But she is ignoring important insights. Oppression based on the expression and exercise of conventional notions of masculinity in sexual relations is not only more subtle and deeper than the overt discrimination practised in the job market, it is often more damaging and demoralizing. Eating disorders, for example, are rampant among girls because of the emphasis placed on women's sexual desirability defined in terms of her conformity to the prevailing body ideal. Disregard for the contribution a woman makes in the home and as a mother can lead to her being badly exploited and treated with contempt. Assumptions about what is 'normal' in sexual relations can lead to instances of harassment and justifications for the use of force and fear. All show the deep way in which personal, emotional and sexual interactions can be an expression of the hostility and contempt directed towards women in an unequal culture.

These are important insights still not fully integrated into perceptions of society, but the politics which flowed from some of these concerns were often highly problematic. The most forceful of these were the anti-sexist, anti-harassment and positive discrimination campaigns in the 1980s. These were about legislating around the perceived relationships of power and oppression. If there had been problems before with applying civil rights rhetoric to the situation between men and women, they certainly got a whole lot worse when applied to these more nebulous areas. Even before drastic changes in sex roles, there were problems with converting perceptions about male power into actual campaigns about personal sexual behaviour and attitudes.

The personal may be political but should the political involve itself with the personal? In the intimate connections between men and women, where attitudes and behaviour are more relevant than economic and legal status, oppression and discrimination become much more difficult to prove. Away from obvious economic and legal discriminations based on gender, the intimate connections between men and women are more muddied by individual differences and lifestyle, by emotional agendas. Prescriptions for appropriate behaviour become difficult in this context. Not all relationships are built on the same chemistry and anyway there is the question of how much the 'feminine' draws out its masculine counterpart. As Barbara Taylor and Sally Alexander pointed out in the *New Statesman* (1980): 'The ropes which bind women are the hardest to cut, because they are woven with so many of our own desires.'

It was the extension of the model of male power into more nebulous aspects of behaviour which eventually lost feminism much of its wider support. But by then feminism was in no mood to consider that its analysis might be ham-fisted and inappropriate for the subtle differences in how individuals negotiate 'masculine' and 'feminine' roles in their own lives. By the mid-1980s, Thatcherism, with its ferocious ideological drive against the 'nanny state', had taken hold. Liberals feared this was an attempt to reverse the changes which had begun to occur in the family and sexual behaviour. They suspected a will to return to a more conventional family which would be available to care for the casualties from a dismembered welfare state. This was not a moment for backsliding. Instead, feminism sought to strengthen alliances with other groups who considered themselves targeted.

The idea that aspects of masculine behaviour could oppress women was an important insight and one which showed that class and material disadvantages were not the only ones that mattered. But it was also a Trojan horse. What came with it were the disaffected, the marginal groups, the 'oppressed' who found a natural home in a movement which defined itself as the rebellion of the oppressed against their oppression. By a giant non-sequitur, the logic ran that if oppression was broader than actual economic discrimination, then any group which felt discriminated against by the status quo must have a home in a movement which had made the subjective experience of oppression a valid basis for not just protest but action. Thus feminism became, in its own words, a 'rainbow alliance' offering a home to any group which considered itself marginal to a white heterosexual male norm: blacks, gays, the disabled. This was in spite of the fact that the sort of discrimination experienced by, for example, a disabled person might have very different roots from the oppression resulting from gender.

My memory of feminism in this period was that it was both exhilarating and mad. Exhilarating because it was a very creative time. Women were not just defining problems for the first time but were constantly coming up with new ideas to improve women's position. Many policies and ideas we now take for granted as objectives of liberal or socialist governments were thrashed out then in workshops and seminars without funding and without formal organizations. Many of the criticisms of the old Labour and its workerist ideologies came first from feminism which spearheaded the idea of democratic alliances. Women freely volunteered their time and energy to attend conferences and workshops to discuss anything and everything which might improve women's position; few imagined there would be any immediate rewards for themselves.

It was also a wildly frustrating time. At this point, feminism attracted some really very disturbed people and the amazing thing in retrospect was how tolerant feminism was of some crazy excesses. Feminists objected to how the tabloid press in the 1980s characterized their activities as being part of the 'loony left', poking fun at the way in which feminism and the Left abased themselves in the face of ever-escalating claims of oppression. But this was not all misrepresentation. At one conference, Linda Bellos, who later mysteriously became leader of Lambeth Council, listed her oppressions to an audience rendered sullen and passive by her superior claims to speak: 'I am black, a woman, lesbian, Jewish, Polish.' 'You are not disabled . . . yet,' countered one participant who still had the energy to protest.

People who were very damaged by personal experiences found a place to feel powerful. The more oppressed they could claim to be, the more right they had to speak. It is no longer heresy to point out how virtually everyone who identified with feminism had some level of problem with male power, for that was the nature of the movement. Autobiographies by women like Gloria Steinem (*Revolution from Within*, 1992) show both how women had problems and why. But there was always a fine line between those who had a problem yet nevertheless kept their eyes on the wider picture, and those who were seeking some kind of compensation for previous damage. It was often difficult to draw that line very clearly. Perhaps those who did most to effect changes for women were creatively damaged, but there must have been enough empathy with those who were seriously damaged for their use of guilt to silence and inhibit others.

What resulted were endless unproductive, unresolved discussions where the logic of the feminist rhetoric of male oppression in the most personal began to emerge. If men are the oppressors, did that mean that any sexual relationship with them was oppressive? Was any male expression of sexual interest the act of a dangerous predator? Was any expression of male sexuality the same as its most brutal expression in crimes like rape? There were some groups of women who answered yes to all these questions. Bonkers, perhaps, but not so wildly out of step that every other feminist silenced them. Rather it was the other way round. Active feminists who lived with men, loved men, had children with them, fell sullenly silent. Life was too short to waste time arguing with your supposed allies when the overarching political culture of the time was so antagonistic.

The weaknesses of the rhetoric which had led logically to this point began to emerge but it didn't stop the bandwagon from rolling on. In the 1980s, partly as a response to the extreme conservatism of the government, there was a mushrooming of radical socialist councils which incorporated much of this rhetoric into their own politics. It was here – looking to America – that the flesh was put on the bones of anti-discrimination and affirmative action policies aimed at challenging prejudice and power in situations which might in the past have been accepted as natural. In England it never quite became strong enough to deserve the title of 'political correctness' but it still appeared to many as an unwarranted intrusion into situations which many people thought were just too diverse and personal to call for such intervention. Had discrimination against women remained blatant, these legislative initiatives might yet have come to fruition, but by the end of the 1980s social and economic realities began to change dramatically. The economy suddenly delivered many of the objectives which feminism had aimed at, even if not quite in the form wanted. This time the arguments about covert discrimination wouldn't quite wash. The world of gender expectations appeared to be turning upside down and feminism had few tools for understanding what had happened.

At the same time as feminism steeled itself to do battle with those intransigent aspects of male behaviour apparently standing in the way of women's progress, the UK economy and society were undergoing seismic changes. Men's economic supremacy, supposedly the basis for all other oppressive behaviour, was crumbling and with it the sex roles originally described by feminism. The widespread support for the conservative values of Thatcherism meant that feminists had failed to recognize the radical changes affecting women's position, let alone to register the changes affecting men. By the 1990s these dramatic upheavals could no longer be missed. When the dust settled, it was clear the gender landscape would never be the same again.

Feminism had come into being to attack a world of male privilege, a world where the economy was driven by male work and where individual homes mirrored this economic reality. In the 1980s this ceased to be true in any simple sense; the sexual composition of the workforce changed out of all recognition. What happened far exceeded any steady incremental increase of women in the labour market. It was so rapid that by the beginning of the 1990s there were as many women working as men. All projections suggest this is a continuing trend; there will soon be more women than men in the workforce.

How had these changes come about? And why did feminists dismiss them as insufficient and pay them such scant attention? The second question is easier to answer. Feminists were much too preoccupied with the superficial lack of change and even the possibility that gains might be reversed. Nor were they alone in missing signs of revolution. Few ordinary citizens understood these changes until they were fully upon us. In the UK most people were bedazzled by the economic boom in the 1980s and failed to notice the deeper changes. This boom was, in fact, underwritten by money raised from selling off North Sea oil resources, thus disguising profound economic difficulties. But at the time, the image of the yuppy, in particular the male stockbroker, embodied a thriving economy. This was also the time when the first images of highly successful career women began to appear, the so-called 'post-feminist career woman', feminists dismissed her as atypical: the city profiteers were just a modern version of an old theme.

In fact, behind the façade of a buoyant economy based on relatively unchanging sexual patterns, long-term changes were dramatically altering the balance of power between the sexes. The generally agreed term now for what has been happening is the 'feminization of the economy'. What it describes is the fact that although the actual number of jobs has remained unchanged since 1970, the types of jobs, the way they are done and who does them have changed. And what is most important here is the change in the ratio of men to women. Women's employment, which had been steadily increasing since the 1970s when the service sector expanded, accelerated in the 1980s at the same time as the number of men employed full-time declined. All in all, since 1970, large numbers of men have left the workforce. There was also a huge increase in the amount of part-time work, much of this going to women. There are now three million more part-time jobs than in the 1970s while, over the same period, men have lost over three million full-time jobs. The proportion of men employed full-time declined from 62 per cent in 1970 to 50 per cent in 1996 (Demos Report, *Tomorrow's Women*, 1997).

These changes in the sexual composition of the workforce were caused by several converging factors in which the ideological contribution of feminism was relatively minor. Feminism certainly made them possible: equal opportunities legislation meant it was no longer legally possible for employers to exclude women from certain jobs, and feminism had broken down social prejudices. Nothing illustrates this more clearly than attitudes towards working mothers. Until feminist values became established, social disapproval made it extremely difficult for middle-class mothers to work. Now the employment rates for mothers is growing faster than the employment rates for women without children. Nearly half of all women with pre-school-age children are working today, compared with a quarter fifteen years ago, a trend which accelerated throughout the 1980s. Between 1985 and 1991, the UK had the fastest rise in employment among women with children under ten in the European Union.

The real engine of this revolution was deeper economic forces. There was a shift from direct production to an economy based on the finance and service sectors which led to the complete closure of certain types of industry, particularly heavy industry. Some traditional male jobs in mining and the steel industry disappeared altogether. Since 1950, five million jobs had gone from industries producing goods. Jobs depending on physical strength, such as construction or the Army, have vanished in their millions. As a consequence of these shifts, in the past fifteen years, two million men have disappeared from the workforce (*Independent*, 2 January 1996). On top of these long-term changes, recession and the development of global markets also played a profound role. Both favoured industries which could shift production from base to base and 'down-size' their workforces at speed in order to stay in business. The result was 'flexibilization', a shift to a culture of short-term contracts, and more part-time work, changes in working patterns which had a profound impact on men.

Actually it is not strictly accurate to talk about the destruction of heavy industry. Those difficult, dirty and arduous industries which relied on skills traditionally associated with men disappeared from the UK but were relocated to the Third World. That sort of work is now performed wherever the production cost is lowest. So Third World countries bear the cost both in environmental terms – the exploitation of their raw materials

– and in terms of human health. In the UK, though, these jobs appear to have gone for good. The jobs in finance and information technology which replaced them are gender-blind, or even favour women because of their dexterity and communication skills. Increasingly big companies have become multinational or global, and prefer to work with part-time or short-term contracts which allow them to move base quickly.

It is hard to say definitively how much the huge increase in women workers, especially part-time women workers, was driven by demand from women themselves for such work and how much by these economic changes. There was probably a meshing of interests. Throughout the 1980s the culture of permanent contracts for full-time jobs gave way to short-term contracts and part-time employment which was both cheaper and more easily dispensed with as companies maintained profit levels in a recession. Certainly women were more prepared for these developments when they came. They were more used to career breaks, had often argued that part-time work might solve childcare problems and had already suggested employers stop valuing unilinear careers and look instead at the overall 'portfolio'. Indeed, feminism had always been vociferous about the way the old male career pattern thwarted human potentiality in both sexes. 'The assumption that people want to change careers, that they want time out of work, that they want to learn new things, go to college, have kids, move in and out of the labour market, rather than stay fixed in one place for forty years, with a gold watch at the end of it, all of those transformations are associated with women' (Bea Campbell, 'Analysis', BBC Radio 4, 1994).

Feminism's interest in increased part-time work and increased flexibility, however, was connected with calls for increased involvement in parenting, and a different relationship between work and home. Such ideas were and remain one of the most significant progressive discourses on how to live in the new millennium, on how to develop new ways of feeling good about yourself and your contribution to society other than just in terms of work achievement. When feminists were vocal about the need for work flexibility, they couldn't have known that global capitalism would deliver the goods quite so promptly and quite so unpleasantly. Nor could they have anticipated that the time at which these arrived would coincide with social developments which whipped the rug out from under men's feet.

Professor Ray Pahl, author of *After Success* (1995), says that men were hit particularly severely by the needs of the global market for job flexibility. The idea of the unilinear career was the basis of masculine identity. It involved sacrifices, either of the body to physical labour or of the soul to the company, to provide for the family. 'Contracting out', 'down-sizing' and 'delayering' meant the end to steady career paths. Some chose self-employment and some had it thrust upon them, but however it arrived, it marked a shift to personal autonomy in the labour market. 'Career ladders' gave way to 'portfolio careers' and men were at first unready. Young men now no longer have those same expectations of traditional jobs for life but it took at least a decade to abandon such expectations. Women, however, were already used to interrupted employment. They had learned to market their diverse skills and demanded praise for balancing home and work. Women 'juggle their lives', *She* magazine proclaimed, coining the ultimate '80s slogan. Many men were unprepared and even unwilling to accept these new conditions when so much of their identity previously rested on traditional careers. There was more at stake for men than women.

As we shall see in the following chapter, there are many who play down the implications of these developments for gender roles or the levelling of the sexes. The increase is in poorly paid, part-time jobs such as retailing, catering and services, so feminization of the workplace just means more poorly paid female employees. This argument does not hold water. In the 1980s it was certainly true that the biggest increase in the numbers of women working was at the lower-paid end, especially in part-time work. But this was no deployment of some reserve army of labour which could be speedily withdrawn at will: this was a shift to more women permanently in the labour market.

This is still not the full story. In the 1990s there has also been a steady increase in the numbers of women working full-time and even at the higher-paid end of the economy. Indeed, women appear to be making dramatic progress in the professions; in 1997, 52 per cent of new solicitors were women; 32 per cent of managers and administrators; 34 per cent of health professionals; and 27 per cent of buyers, brokers and sales reps (Demos Report, *Tomorrow's Women*, 1997). Given that professional jobs are growing faster than any other occupational group, with women forecast to have 44 per cent of those jobs by 2001, this does not sound as if women are confined to the poorly-paid sector. With girls currently outperforming boys at school and universities, the education gap is also closing and women are likely to be more highly qualified than men. 'The high skill end of the economy . . . is finding as many candidates among young women as young men and since the mid-eighties . . . it has been jobs for women in the full-time sector, in the professional and technical occupations, that have been on the increase' (Heather Joshi, interview with author, 1998).

Women's increased role in the economy means that women have more personal wealth than ever before. Two-income families, while often necessary to deal with rising costs, now have great advantages over one-income families. The number of women earning more than their partners has trebled from 1 in 15 in the early 1980s to 1 in 5 by the mid-1990s. Among childless couples with degrees, it is normal for women to provide half the income. In 1996 it was estimated that more than 20 per cent of couples had the woman as the main breadwinner (*Focus*, March 1998). Women have also made inroads into the corridors of power. There are more women on boards than ever before, and a larger number of women running successful businesses. These are the statistics behind the fact that, for most educated couples now, sexual equality at all levels of life is simply taken for granted.

Although many of these changes may appear to affect only

the higher paid, it does not mean they are any the less significant. The old feminist equation that being a woman *necessarily* entails low income and low status is no longer always true, even if it sometimes is. Feminists cannot have it both ways. Maybe not all women are in well-paid full-time jobs, and maybe it is still more usual for women to be in low-paid part-time work, but not all are, and nor do they of necessity have to be. So one of the vital foundations of feminist argument – that women are always financially disadvantages – has been seriously shaken. As we have seen in the previous chapters, these economic changes also coincided with changes in law and morality which mean that, for the first time in recorded history, women have at least in theory the opportunity to be economically autonomous and to earn money at the same level as their male counterparts. These developments cannot be dismissed just because the poorest women are still at the bottom of the heap; if feminism was premised on the idea that women are always structurally disadvantaged, what happens to that premise if it is no longer true?

In theory these developments do not necessarily have any implications for the relative position of the sexes, but at the beginning of the 1990s, as the recession deepened, the public began to notice the differential effect of these changes on men and women. In the past, a recession would have signalled that the part-time, less protected workforce was about to be laid off. On this occasion, it was the full-time 'men's jobs' which went. At first this was picked up by the media as a temporary phenomenon, the stuff of a classic recession. They began to describe the estates where men hung about idle and depressed, and to interview men who stayed at home while their women worked. Rioting in the early 1990s on several estates in Newcastle, Cardiff and Oxford drew attention to something worse – dangerous anger rooted in enforced idleness. Gradually recognition filtered through that there were communities in which traditional forms of male employment might never return.

Once questions had been asked about how these changes were affecting men and women rather than how they were affecting communities or families or different social classes, it was impossible not to notice that men and women had gradually been affected in opposite ways. Endless articles in the 1980s had documented high-achieving women and women's new economic and social clout. This had been, in the media cliché, the 'women's decade', with Margaret Thatcher delivering the message that nothing stood between a determined woman and her ambitions. The fact that the markets suddenly began to deliver the kinds of work and working patterns for which feminists had campaigned added to the perception that women were on a roll. Simultaneously, though more difficult to prove, individual women seemed to be buoyed up by a sense of overthrowing the old obstacles to women's achievements and suddenly finding themselves the prototype employee for global capitalism.

By the late 1980s men were appearing in the opposite light. The huge increase in male unemployment, both in heavy industrial and small businesses, accompanied by visible signs of recession, suddenly revealed men as disproportionately affected. Psychologically they were unprepared. The media began to note the effect on households where unemployed men refused to consider taking 'demeaning' women's jobs as well as refusing to help in the home while the women struggled with both. Feminism had given women the confidence to move into masculine areas, combining work and motherhood, seeing new opportunities in new work patterns. Men, by contrast, were experiencing their work changes, this so-called feminization of labour, more like a smack in the eye.

Evidence of male difficulties came from every quarter, including statistics on suicide and male homelessness. It also came from the so-called lucky ones, the employed. Frustration and resentment were rife, especially over any calls for positive discrimination. The Equal Opportunities Commission began to receive complaints from men; by the mid-1990s it was receiving more complaints from men than women.

The concept of a male backlash does not begin to address what was happening here. A report published in 1995 by

Parents in Work showed that men were suffering from very real insecurity, not some imagined loss of prestige. Britain had the longest working hours in Europe and the lowest productivity. Some feminists joked about these statistics; they proved women's suspicions that overtime is often empty macho time, an ethos expressed clearly in an advertisement for an engineering firm spotted by Professor Pahl: 'people with outside interests need not apply.' But these long, unproductive hours were evidence of a desperate desire to hold on to jobs at all costs. At the time, Ray Pahl said: 'People are scared of not being seen as good workers although in a rapidly changing market, they are not clear what that means. The traditional male career has collapsed. One response is extreme competitiveness, ruthlessness about getting to the top and getting vast salaries. But the other is anxiety and even disillusionment about work altogether.' According to surveys conducted in the mid-1990s, such distrust and anxiety was endemic, a crisis of confidence which spread across all classes and age groups (Demos Report, *No Turning Back*, 1995).

Demos, the left-liberal think-tank which conducted a survey of attitudes among eighteen- to twenty-four-year-olds, elsewhere referred to these changes as merely 'women's enhanced role in the economy' (*Tomorrow's Women*, 1997), a gradual evolution towards a more level playing field. The public, however, did not always see it that way. By the time knowledge of these changes entered public consciousness, they already had a particular spin on them, connected with general anxieties about society and what was happening to the family. None of this was happening in isolation. Other social changes were pushing men into the forefront of social concerns: recession and unemployment; depression and school failure; changing family patterns; the increase in violent crime with young men as both its perpetrators and victims; and a preoccupation with yobs and their ever-younger counterparts, 'evil-boys'. Each crisis further undermined the old feminist way of viewing men as potentates. Increasingly they were appearing as both cause and symptom of a society in crisis.

Perhaps these economic changes would not have been taken up as so critical for men had they not coincided with growing insecurities about the family. However, they were experienced by most ordinary people as part and parcel of difficult times. When Britain entered the 1990s, it entered a dark period both socially and politically. Scarcely a day went past without news of ever more shocking acts of violence and immorality: stories of increasing lawlessness, joy-riding, riots on estates, drunken violence and property destruction. Many of these stories concerned younger and younger children. There were twelve-year-olds who had killed children when their stolen car veered out of control; there were lawless youngsters intimidating estates; there were thirteen-year-olds accused of rape. Kenneth Clarke, then Home Secretary, vowed that his government would deal with 'nasty persistent, juvenile little offenders'. This violence among children seemed to symbolize a rot which had spread from adults into the very core of society. In February 1993 came the ultimate tragedy – the murder of two-year-old James Bulger, abducted, tortured and sadistically killed by two ten-year-old boys.

Jamie Bulger's murder was set against the background of the changing economy and the changes in domestic life. For many it was the apotheosis of a time out of joint. It signified the ruin of old communities, of poverty and increasingly harsh conditions. Above all, it was seen as a crisis of morality, a moment when we were invited to ask whether we were rearing monsters. 'The case fills us', said A. N. Wilson in the *Evening Standard*, 'with the uneasy dread that this horrifying crime is somehow symptomatic of something which has happened to our society at large.' The Bulger murder came to symbolize what happens in a society of divorced parents, single mothers, unemployed fathers, drunkenness, and no authority or discipline. 'Few can doubt the family is in trouble,' pronounced the *Sunday Times* in March 1993. 'Parliament and the people are now casting around for solutions to what is seen as a problem of epidemic disorder – rising crime, intrusive squalor, spreading welfare dependency, collapsed community.' This anxiety about the family would frame all further discussion of gender roles.

Of course, ever since the first stirrings of feminism there had been a vocal minority who warned of the dire consequences of women's push for greater economic and legal autonomy from the family. But even in the heyday of Thatcher this remained a relatively marginal, backward-looking position. If one dares use old Marxist terms, libertarian and feminist views were still 'hegemonic', meaning that the emphasis was still on the obstacles to women's full independence, and crime and social disorder were still seen as stemming from poverty and hardship not from the disintegration of the traditional family.

Increasingly, however, politicians of both Left and Right began to express concern that many social problems had their source in the demise of the traditional family and men's dis-placement within that. 'Across the political, moral, intellectual and religious spectrum there is today agreement that small, warm, caring families are the one way of virtually guaranteeing that children do not end up as criminals, but they seem to be a dying breed. The abnormal family seems now to be the norm' (*Sunday Times* 1993). As Shadow Home Secretary Tony Blair said in 1992: 'There is something very wrong with our society ... criminals of 10 or 11 don't just happen. Broken homes, bad housing, poor education, no job or training, lack of hope or opportunity – affect the way a child develops.'

Clearly, optimism about the liberalizing changes of the 1960s and '70s – including the vast improvements in women's position – had unravelled. The 'enhanced role' of women in the econ-omy was not seen in isolation but alongside everything else. Some feminists continued to focus on further obstacles to their advancement, their freedoms, but this old story of the male oppressor no longer resonated in the same way, no longer 'galvanised the imagination' as Liam Hudson has put it (*TLS* March 1998). In the popular imagination, what was taking hold was the problem of male redundancy not the problem of too much male power or too little male support for women. The tabloids were full of stories like that of the father who, 'tor-mented by separation', killed his four children, and they showed increasing sympathy for those divorced men who felt they were being kept from their children.

By contrast, the female side of the disintegrated family – the single mother – assumed an ever more monstrous appearance. She became someone who chose not to have a regular male partner and lived on state benefits. Mrs Thompson, the mother of one of the boys who killed James Bulger, thereby creating the 'brutalized children of the wasteland', was painted in just this light. 'It is always someone else's fault – not hers for being drunk and argumentative, nor for having a succession of relationships with different men' (*Evening Standard*, November 1993). Throughout the 1990s she became a media cliché. In this context feminism's rhetoric about male oppression appeared to deliver a double whammy, kicking men on their way down, wresting power and advantages from those who are already diminished.

Feminism's rallying cry of 'having it all', with which career women had heralded their push into the labour market, subtly changed to a cry of greed. Popular concern was no longer with what more could be done to advance women's cause, but with what was happening to men. Doubts were raised about how fully men participated within the family and questions were asked about what would happen as a result of their displacement from it. In part, the changes affecting family law and welfare provision had made it seem as if women could in theory float free from men, undermining the previously unquestioned assumption that the male role in the family was an economic one.

These anxieties had striking parallels with the critical importance given to every change affecting women in the 1960s and '70s. But then women were at the spearhead of exciting social changes in the economy, in family values and especially in gender relations. Now the changes affecting men seemed to put them at the blunt end. In language which flew in the face of the feminist mantras of women's oppression, the talk now was of male 'crisis', 'underachievement', 'failure', even 'redundancy'. 'The Descent of Man' was a headline used by several newspapers examining the situation. In February 1994 the *Daily Express* put forward what was now becoming a common line of questioning in a series on 'The Obsolete Male': had women taken something away from men as they made gains? And where did that leave men?

4   THE FULL MONTY

The economic changes of the 1980s and '90s amounted to a revolution, some of it achieved in response to feminism's demands, some delivered by the needs of an entirely new economy. A world was created in which many of the old work patterns disappeared for good. What has emerged is not exactly the world dreamt of by feminists – a world of easy sharing and mutual fulfilment – but then again neither is it the world feminists originally set out to attack. It is no longer a world where men dominate the economic activity of the country or monopolize power, nor does 'the family' automatically imply a male breadwinner and a dependent wife repressed emotionally and sexually and struggling to retain a separate identity.

This is a new order where gender does not have the same significance. It is no longer true to say that because of her gender a woman will automatically be economically disadvantaged. Many women now reach levels of income and power previously the exclusive territory of men, so old assumptions about differential incomes reflecting men's greater power no longer work. This has muddied the old social divisions. In many cases, families with two professional incomes – the offensively termed 'work-rich households' – have enormous advantages over those where only one partner works, or indeed where both partners are on low incomes. Unemployment, a low-income family, reliance on benefit and single parenthood are much more important in determining an individual's economic status than gender. Not to mention that other aspects of our lives are probably just as important in determining how many opportunities or how much fulfilment is to come our way. Factors such as ethnic background, relationship to the cultural and intellectual elite, and the quality of one's immediate environment are all divisions which now condition life's expectations as much as gender.

Of course, class and other social divisions have always existed and some socialists always believed they were more important than gender. But, in the past, evidence of discrimination against women was so compelling and visible that even the most hard-line socialists realized it was churlish to downplay the facts. In pre-feminist days, if a woman found herself without a partner, through death, divorce or failure to marry, her gender would always put her in a position of hardship. That no longer has to happen. Women are no longer in the doll's house – permanently limited, infantilized and unhappy because of dependency on men. So now those other social divisions, and a myriad new ones, often seem much more important than gender.

Definitive evidence of change is the fact that now it is men as much as women who occupy positions which previously proved discrimination against women. Twenty-five years ago men did better in education, got the higher status jobs and even sometimes received preferential legal treatment. Throughout the 1990s evidence of male difficulty poured in from every side. In the 1960s, for instance, feminists pointed to girls' inferior educational performance as proof they had internalized assumptions about social inferiority. By 1996 girls at primary school were shown doing better than boys. Similarly, when tested at sixteen, girls outperformed boys in every subject. At primary school 92 per cent of those excluded are boys, as are 80 per cent at secondary school. Aged sixteen, there are 15 per cent of boys receiving no education at all compared with only 12 per cent of girls. Only 67 per cent of boys continue with education compared with 73.8 per cent of girls. The newspaper article which spelt out these trends, summed them up: 'Girls are better than Boys. Official' (*Observer*, January 1998). So if in the 1990s boys have been consistently performing less well at school than girls and having far more problems within the education system, does it mean they are now internalizing messages of inferiority?

Other areas confirm that it is no longer women who are automatically disadvantaged or positioned as victims. Men might be more likely to commit a crime but they are also more likely to be its victims, twice as likely as women in fact to be the victims of violent crime. Young men are particularly vulnerable: 53 per cent of victims of violent street crime are men in their twenties, and males aged between ten and twenty are twice as likely as girls to be attacked. In July 1998, figures confirmed that in the UK men were more likely to be unemployed than women, to be precise 50 per cent more likely. The discrepancy is even more remarkable among the long-term unemployed. Men make up 70 per cent of those unemployed for more than a year and 80 per cent of those unemployed for more than two years. The article which reported these statistics added: 'It's probably no coincidence that men are nine times more likely than women to be homeless and three times more likely to commit suicide' (*Observer*, 19 July 1998).

Recent statistics about the family also cast an odd light on that old notion of male tyranny. In the past women railed against their lack of rights in the family, deriving from a time when the patriarch had been able to initiate divorce and retain control over children and property. Now, if the protests of some fathers are to be believed, the opposite is true. In the 1990s, 75 per cent of all divorces were initiated by women and the majority of these women remained in the home and gained custody of the children. In 1996, Dave Cohen wrote: 'In the family – the traditional bastion of male power – the financial independence of women means that they are no longer prepared to take the nonsense they used to, leading to a doubling of the number of women petitioning their husbands for divorce in the past 20 years' (*Guardian* Weekend, 4 May 1996).

All in all these are dramatic changes which appear to have put men in the same critical position occupied by women twenty years previously when feminism erupted as the voice of their disaffection. Yet it has proved almost impossible to look at these changes in any clear-headed way. No sooner had the changes been noticed than they were packaged up into the notion of 'crisis' – a notion either to be milked to death or vehemently rejected. 'Fearful, anxious, vociferous and sometimes violent,' ran one headline in the *Independent* (2 January 1996). 'Meet the new victims of the Nineties: Men.'

As we saw in the previous chapters, media attention to these changes came mainly in the form of a comparison between the different trajectories of the sexes: 'The future is female is a slogan that goes with the grain of so many current trends,' says Dave Hill, author of *The Future of Men* (1997). 'As girls do better and better at school, boys trail behind; as women secure more and better jobs, men become intimate with the schedules of daytime t.v.; while men kill themselves with increasing frequency, women lead lives that are not only longer but sweeter.' Fay Weldon concurs: 'Girls are having a better life. They do better at school, gain more qualifications, give you less lip, find it easier to get jobs, are better able to live without men than men can live without women' (Interview with author, 1998).

Scarcely missing a beat, the focus shifted to doom-laden scenarios about the future of men, and questions of role reversal or even redundancy. The nineties, claimed the *Independent* (2 January 1996), seems 'to be dominated by men trying to be more like women . . . Their jobs are no longer as secure as they were, if they exist at all. Demand for their work or home skills is declining. They are increasingly prone to violence. Women seem ever more confident and able to do without them.' The *Daily Express* ran a special series in February 1994 on 'The Obsolete Male'. The *Daily Mail* ran a similar one, 'The Redundant Male', in March 1996.

New developments in reproductive technology provided a handy metaphor for what was happening to men. Fatherhood, said Melanie Phillips, 'has been reduced to an emission in a test tube . . . Thanks to the wonders of reproductive technology, women can now do without a male presence altogether' (*Observer*, 2 November 1997). She concludes that their need for social participation is similarly reduced by women's autonomy.

There's a new category, said one commentator, 'the unemploy-able, unmarriageable male'. 'Unless men change,' warned Dave Cohen, 'the collective evidence seems to suggest they could become economically, socially and biologically redundant' (*Guardian* Weekend, 4 May 1996).

It is not hard to see why, in a society awash with such meta-phors, *The Full Monty* became one of the most successful films in British cinema history. Not because, as many critics said, it creates a 'feel-good factor', although the mood is ultimately upbeat when the group of downtrodden men who become strippers refuse to accept as inevitable their total unem-ployability or the break-up of their marriages, but more because the film taps in precisely to these very '90s' preoccupations with men's role and male redundancy. The base-line of the film is clear when the main characters discuss their predicament at a jobcentre in Sheffield, 'We're not needed any more. We're obsolete. Dinosaurs,' says the central character.

This is a much bleaker film than *Brassed Off*, another British film dealing with a community devastated by the closure of its main industry. Indeed, Channel 4 invested in the script development of both films. Faced with having to make a choice they went with *Brassed Off* and put *The Full Monty* into turn-around, becoming the only company to lose money on the film. The difference between the two films relates to their portrayal of sexual relationships. Although made in the 1990s, *Brassed Off* is a very 1980s film. It too deals with redundancy, this time among a group of miners. Yet this film still has an old-fashioned left-wing agenda: management's inhumanity to its workers and male prejudice. The drama consists of the men having to over-come their prejudice against a woman joining their colliery band, especially as she turns out to be a member of the hated management.

The Full Monty appeared only two years later but seems a world away. It was *The Full Monty* which galvanized the imagina-tion rather than *Brassed Off*, because it belongs to the new landscape of the disappearance of traditional male jobs and of gender reversal. In *Brassed Off*, the male miners chuckle over having inappropriately talked of 'women pissing in the wind'. 'Can they do that?' asks one of the miners. The exchange is intended to show up the lingering sexism towards and ignorance about women. In *The Full Monty*, the women even symbolically assume the male position, standing up to take a piss. And the film ends with the men economically powerless as women used to be, selling the only thing they have: their bodies. It captured the prevailing mood because what people are really engaging with now is not ignorant sexism (which they can deal with) but how men are going to live in a world of independent women.

Whether you believe that men really are in crisis or not, it is obvious from this widespread preoccupation with male crises and redundancy that, at the very least, a large tranche of the public believe we are living through a gender revolution. Most people acknowledge that men's and women's roles have undergone massive changes, and that the outcome varies from uncertain to catastrophic. Most eyes are also focused on men and boys, and their precarious future, not on what women can do to improve their lot. Typically, one mother wrote to a tabloid in 1997:

> The alienation of working class boys today . . . is real. As a mother of three working class boys I've felt for a long time their needs are being ignored. Many traditional manufacturing jobs no longer exist and many family-minded girls would rather have no resident father for their children than an unemployed or low-paid lad who eats them out of house and home.

So how have feminists responded to such a broadside on fundamental tenets? By deciding it is time to re-examine feminism in this new context? By deciding that feminist ideas and policies need a thorough overhauling to see what remains relevant? By facing up to what is going on and trying to understand it? By sorting out fact from fantasy without preconceptions? Have they heck! By and large the response has been one of scorn, focusing not on the real changes and their meanings but on finding fault with the public response to these issues. Feminists have spent far more time on disputing the idea that men are in trouble than on trying to understand the implications of contemporary changes or what people are worrying about. Far more time is spent on criticizing the moral agenda that now enters into any consideration of the family than on trying to understand the basis for public fears about these family changes.

There are some feminist-inspired commentators who have charted society from the point of view of gender, often brilliantly, but there are many more clinging on to the old concepts, especially in politics, social policy and academia. There has been a collective reluctance to submit the whole area to scrutiny, and a widespread refusal to see this talk of crisis as anything other than sexist scare-mongering. Instead of accepting that the old 'truths' of feminism are due for an overhaul, numerous attempts are made to breathe life into the old concepts and politics. This is somewhat worrying since women who think like this now have more influence than ever before in many western governments.

The most common response is 'Crisis, what crisis?' These are not real changes but misperceptions arising from deep sexism. Observations about men's changed status are really squeals of masculine protest against their loss of economic power and prestige. 'It's only when gender contrasts appear in ways which seem to question the traditional assumption that men should be the dominant sex, that media attention is focused upon them,' says Lynn Segal. Attention to boys' underachievement in exams is 'typical'. Educationalist Professor Caroline Gipps says that it took years to get attention and action for girls' underachievement, but that it has been almost instantaneous when it affects boys. (Interview for 'Analysis', Radio 4, March 1998)

Other feminists assert that if there are changes, they are superficial. In *Who's Afraid of Feminism? Seeing through the Backlash* (1997), Juliet Mitchell and Anne Oakley argue that these changes are 'cosmetic', denying that this constitutes any real equality or potency for women. Helen Wilkinson argues in *Tomorrow's Women* (Demos Report, 1997) that these changes are not so significant because although there has been a steady increase in women's employment, 'the majority of women are in low status work'.

Natasha Walter in *The New Feminism* (1998) calls on women to remember at all costs the material 'facts' of women's continuing disadvantages. In similar vein, the American Virginia Valian insists in *Why So Slow?* (1998), we should focus on the continuing 'unfairness' of women's position. Polly Toynbee summed up this belief that men are still massively advantaged and powerful compared with women when she claimed that, for the majority of women,

> Life is as hard a struggle as ever. Twenty years after the equal pay act women still earn 20% less than men. Women are clustered at the bottom of every ladder, if there's a ladder out at all. Most women work but their jobs are not liberating, as part-time carers and caterers, squeezing jobs into unsocial hours to fit in with their families for whom they still overwhelmingly provide all the care and housework. (*Guardian*, 26 May 1998)

So however many women workers there are now, these contemporary feminists believe they remain exploited and underpaid because so many of them, especially mothers, are part-time. And part-time work shows how much women are being held back from achieving full equality by their domestic obligations, especially if men don't do their bit around the home.

At one level these views may seem reasonable. If the issue is examined exclusively from the point of view of economic earnings and political position – making the comparison by way of averages – then it is still the case that women's average income remains only 75 per cent of men's, that women are still massively absent from senior management, and that, in spite of Blair's 101 new women MPs, they also remain a minority in formal politics and in the most powerful institutions in the country.

If you add to this the evidence that women still bear the burden of domestic responsibilities, that women's freedom of movement is restricted by fear of male violence, that domestic violence mainly affects women, and that women are in many contexts still exposed to dismissive and disparaging attitudes, the suggestion of men losing power to women seems patently absurd. And even where women's economic gains seem undeniable, writers like this insist that on balance these changes have actually further disadvantaged women: the increase in women working, given that much of it is low-paid, combined with their continued primary responsibility for the home, has created a double burden. Women are suffering because they want to be equal but men are unwilling to shift in their masculine identity.

Behind these reasonable reassertions of the 'material' reality of women's oppression there is inflexibility and real evasion. Of course there is no getting around the fact that combining work with the primary responsibility for home and children does create terrible strains. But that's neither the end of the story nor the only story. Feminists are refusing to look at data on the economy and gender division, and especially what ordinary people might be feeling about this, in any light which would undermine fundamental beliefs about the multiple disadvantages of women. It reduces all and any protest by or about men and their current difficulties to a backlash against having had to give up powers. 'If you are hearing men's cry of pain,' says Polly Toynbee, 'don't listen.'

This really is not good enough. It is extremely contemptuous of and insensitive to people's worries. As the rest of this book argues, this is not whether women are earning 20 per cent less on average than men; much more they are concerned with renegotiating gender roles in a new landscape, with how to make the right choices about family and work, and with quality of life issues which are as much to do with the state of society and the environment as they are to do with pay differentials.

Nor is it just a matter of gender differentials no longer galvanizing the wider populace to address an urgent injustice; it is also that these contemporary feminists are wilfully refusing to acknowledge changes in gender roles as anything but an illusion. Yet, as I have suggested earlier, gender is no longer determining employment and social position as it previously did. In 1996, Professor Heather Joshi found in a study of twenty-six-year-olds that:

> It didn't really matter whether they were male or female, it mattered a lot what their class backgrounds had been and how well educated they had been and if they had been unemployed as teenagers. But ten years ago gender would have been a terrific discriminator. Or twenty years previously, half the women had already dropped out of employment at twenty-six. ('Analysis', Radio 4, March 1998)

In other words, gender is becoming dramatically less significant in determining the levels and patterns of a full-time career than it would have been even ten years ago. Joshi's work is that of a painstaking academic economist so she gives the old-fashioned feminists' let-out clause: she says her findings are not yet conclusive. Perhaps, she says, these same women may yet drop out or reduce career expectations when they have families, although she insists that the very dramatic career dips of yester-year are now disappearing.

But even if the majority of women continue to downgrade their career expectations after the birth of children, or work part-time to fit in with children's needs, is this really evidence of women's continued oppression, especially now when it is so much easier and acceptable for mothers to work? If they do drop out is it only the lack of affordable, available childcare holding them back? Catherine Hakim, a sociologist, agrees that the economy has been 'feminized' but only because of the increase in numbers of women working part-time: 'These women are secondary earners, they are supplementing the husband's wage, nothing very much has changed in the sexual division of labour in the family. They're still responsible for the children primarily and . . . social surveys make it quite clear that's an agreed choice those couples are making' ('Analysis', March 1998).

In rejecting the feminist complaint that women have no choice, Hakim swings to the other extreme, upholding a voluntarist model. She thinks women choose from a very early age whether they want to prioritize career or children or combine them, and claims that surveys consistently show one-third of all women taking up each of these choices. When career women suddenly change their minds and leave work, it is because 'women are spectacularly bad at making up their own minds'.

Ultimately, Hakim seems to rely on the idea of personality types with preferences, claiming there will always be certain types of women who want to stay at home. So is it feminine muddle-headedness which often sends women off down the wrong path? This preference theory seems hopelessly inadequate as an account of why people chose to do what they do, how conformity is extracted and how people can and do change. But fundamentally she is only reinforcing what others – including myself in *Our Treacherous Hearts* (1992) – had already noted, that some women are genuinely choosing to prioritize home and children not just being forced to do so by the labour market. Sometimes decisions are to do with quality of life: either women are privileged enough to have a choice, or they value time with children above the strains of full-time employment even if it means economic hardship.

Whatever the precise reason, it signals a degree of choice for women which up to very recently most men have not considered available to them. Now there is less social prejudice against men staying at home with the children, it is no longer uncommon for men to chose to do so, but feminists have been remarkably narrow-minded about accepting that this choice might feel attractive once the old family structures began to break down. Instead, the loudest feminist voice in the family debate has been the continuing complaint about the double burden of childcare and work. The most common statistics wheeled out prove how little time the working father spends with his children and how much of the work in the home still falls to women.

'Why doesn't man want to do his share?' moans Virginia Valian in her book *Why So Slow?* (1998). 'In the workplace slackers exist, but they are looked down on by others.' So this feminism insists the family is still a place of subordination and personal restriction, even though the economic edifice on which that model was built is crumbling.

Interpretation of employment statistics and family trends is only one part of the problem. Many feminists have refused to acknowledge any real grounds for worry behind the widespread moral panic about the family. Instead they insist all talk of crisis and disintegration has unfairly scapegoated women, especially single mothers, and feminism. You can see why they might be defensive when the likes of Lynda Lee Potter writes: 'By single mothers . . . I mean those who got pregnant despite not having a home, income, or steady chap. Women who think it's their right to have several children by itinerant men and expect us to support them in perpetuity' (*Daily Mail*, 4 June 1997). This is just denouncing single mothers in the most stereotyped and offensive terms without any understanding of the reality of their lives, but to respond to such bigotry and ignorance with defensiveness does not really help. Leaving aside imaginary bogeywomen, there is a discussion to be had about why many men are absent from families and whether this is because they wish to be or because women no longer feel they need them. There's also a discussion to be had about what a father can and should give to his children. Yet feminism's silence on these subjects has been deafening.

There are also wider questions about women in the economy which feminism has ignored altogether. In the UK the move to two-income families has been part of a wider social shift, in particular the expansion of the middle classes. Dual incomes are about buying into, or staying afloat, in a certain lifestyle which in this country is very much connected with holidays, cars, consumer goods and private housing. For low-income families a woman's work can mean the difference between survival in this lifestyle or not; for high earners, a second income can mean great affluence. Taken overall, the increase of two-income families has underpinned the expansion of the middle classes, opening up lifestyles previously closed to working-class families.

No one would want to go back to a situation where women were deprived of choice and had fewer rights than men to seek satisfaction through work, but relentless economic growth based on consumerism does have costs, especially for our own and others' environments. It has meant more travel, more cars, more pollution, but some feminists view it as heresy to link the expansion of women's employment with negative aspects of unlimited consumer growth. Occasionally, though, women, feeling like hamsters in a wheel running to keep still, do wonder whether they have been recruited into an economy whose ultimate unsustainability is already undermining any advantages which dual incomes might bring.

Economic issues such as these – the impact of consumer growth on the environment, the way dual-income families feed into other social divisions, the question of whether women really want to work in the same way as men while their children are small – are taboo in feminist thinking. Yet many ordinary women know that decisions about the family and work are complex and do not really fit into the old feminist mantras of financial independence, the right to be the breadwinner, the need for full-time childcare. That is why so few of them can get worked up about the idea of reviving feminism and why many are cynical about the insistence of the now highly successful old-fashioned feminists that special pleading for women is still crucial.

One social issue highlights all this. Demands for the separate taxation of men and women made perfect sense in the context of a political movement to establish women's autonomy. Not only was there a clear ethical case against women being treated as adjuncts of their husbands, there was also a need to overthrow a system which treated women as second class. Feminists also believed that without this separation of finances, money in the household could be distributed unfairly, to the disadvantage of women. Anna Coote summed up this view while opposing the idea of restoring joint taxation: 'It would signal that somehow the family is a cosy, consensual institution, whereas in fact there are lots of households with rich men and poor women, and where there is a lot of conflict' (*Guardian*, 2 June 1997).

I can remember those sentiments once felt like an important cornerstone of feminism. I even used voluntarily to spend weekends at seminars discussing taxation, and felt passionately that it was wrong that my income should in any way be merged with my partner's. Maybe this was because I can remember parental rows when my mother started working. Both parents were equally thrown, but for different reasons, when her earnings were deducted from his income. What their rows exposed was the whole fraught idea of income distribution within the family and, like many other women at that time, I viewed it as an indignity, an inequality, an outrage that women did not have full autonomy in income and taxation.

These assertions look different now. Not because there's anything wrong with the spirit of autonomy in income, but this particular policy now mainly benefits high-income families, not necessarily women in general. As equality has increased between partners, the problem of injustices in controlling domestic resources may be less pronounced. In such circumstances, the main beneficiaries are wealthy families where both are working. Richard Thomas has called it, 'a terrific boon for the super-wealthy' who are able to 'shift investment income into the name of a non-earning or low-earning spouse thus avoiding punitive tax rates' (*Guardian*, 2 June 1997).

Independent taxation for men and women makes it hard to reform child benefit by linking it through taxation to family income. The fact that women can be low earners in wealthy families means that while taxation is kept separate and child benefit goes to the mother, there is no way of getting an accurate picture of household income. Importantly, this separate taxation is also stopping governments from raising the tax threshold to raise more revenue. If a tax threshold is set exclusively based on individual income, it is not fair to raise the level of taxation. If a family has only one earner with dependent spouse and kids, an income of, say, £25,000 is not enormous and further taxation would be difficult. But a household where both individuals are earning £25,000 would be able to afford more taxation, even if reluctantly.

What is at stake here is a shift in perspective. In the 1970s, the campaign for separate taxation, which culminated in changed rules in the late 1980s, made perfect sense because it was addressing a perceived injustice between men and women. But in the 1990s, when women have generally a more equitable economic position, and in the context of other social divisions, this injustice between men and women does not seem overwhelmingly more significant than the injustices between different families. Richard Thomas continues: 'there is a problem now which is more pressing than the gap between men and women: the horrifying soul-destroying gap between rich and poor. Removal of independent taxation would make it easier to take more cash off the rich.' He adds that the biggest obstacle to making changes is political, 'middle-class women in particular view independent taxation as a cornerstone of their new higher status'.

When feminism emerged, the fight for independence and autonomy was part of an all-out attack on the male-dominated family which stood as an obstacle to both a woman's self-development and her economic independence. The pursuit of autonomy and independence, however, while profoundly egalitarian in its intent, is in certain areas now adding to the power and wealth of certain women and their families. Some of feminism's fundamental tenets aimed at redressing inequalities between men and women may now be adding to the widening gulfs between rich and poor, between unemployed and employed, between different communities. So terrified are liberal governments of these feminist principles that they would rather do anything than contravene them. Thus, in the supposedly 'women's budget' of 1998, Gordon Brown focused on incentives for getting women on benefits into work. Controversial though these measures were, they were a lot safer than anything which would have forced wealthy women to examine how the system was working in their favour.

If feminism is sceptical about the idea of changing economic realities for women, it has been positively contemptuous about the notion of men's social and emotional difficulties. Indeed, less tangible signs of a male crisis are invariably interpreted as men's reluctance to give up their power. Male depression, uncertainty about roles, difficulties in the family, anti-social behaviour, all become 'backlash' phenomena: protests, inflexibility, dinosaur behaviour. It has even been claimed that the 1990s has seen men reasserting that old authority over women, a celebration of so-called laddishness and a rejection of anything that smacked of 'new' (i.e. pro-feminist) maleness. 'On the face of it,' says Susie Orbach, 'things now look better for women and girls (and in some ways they are) but the general climate in which sexual politics is discussed means "New man" is derided, "Laddishness" is condoned and women seen as sexual objects.' Germaine Greer, in her new book, says it is time for women to get angry again. Far from having too much taken away from them, men have not yet given up enough.

This idea of masculine protest means that feminists are seeing the male side of changes – just like the female side – as an illusion. Men only *appear* disproportionately affected by social changes. What is really going on is their reluctance to let go the moral authority conferred by masculine status. Men are dangerous creatures still because, whatever else has changed, they have not yielded their moral authority. And so long as this remains intact they will find any opportunity to reassert their potency. Such assumptions obviate the need for rethinking feminist aims or objectives because the fundamentals remain the same. Men are still powerful (despite local disadvantages) and women are still structurally disadvantaged because masculinity still carries more weight and authority.

Recently Fay Weldon caused a little stir by challenging this. Unfortunately, she took issue by reversing the evidence. If women are not the oppressed, then men must be. 'Men are the new victims now,' she claims. 'I can see that I grew up as

a persecuted woman, a depressed woman and that was something you could fight about and measure and see and resist
and demand equality and sisterhood and equal wages and a
sort of equal ability to look after your own children' ('Analysis',
Radio 4, March 1998). Now she thinks men are in that position.
'Men start to feel as women used to feel about men 30 years ago.
If only I'd been born one of those.' Polly Toynbee promptly
dismissed this as 'nonsense about how powerful women are
destroying men' (*Guardian*, 6 May 1998).

This mud–slinging about which sex is most oppressed is a
pointless waste of time. Both sides are hanging on to old ways
of thinking about gender relations as a simple relation of power,
one sex over the other, arguing about who has the upper hand
now, which sex is the victim sex, and whether these changes
are illusions. None of which enables us to find out what has
really been going on. What is needed now is a much freer
way of looking at the crisis; the old ways are misleading and
damaging.

As will become clear in the rest of this book, there are other,
less obvious elements currently at play in the debate about
gender, especially changing class relations. Worries about boys
and men may ultimately need to be understood less in terms
of gender and more in terms of public fears of 'contamination
by mass culture', together with fears of moral disintegration
and anxieties about how families will live and cope. In the
remainder of this book, I am going to look more closely at
some of the areas where masculinity is said to be in crisis. In
almost every area fundamental feminist propositions have been
reasserted. As a result, the huge transformations – economic,
social and emotional – which have been rocking our society
have been skated over, often forced back into clichéd interpretations.

A much more complex picture emerges when we take these
areas separately without old-fashioned feminist preconceptions.
Gender is still important but not uniformly so. In some areas
there is discrimination against women, in some areas against
men. But in many of these areas women themselves can often

be found resisting change or failing to adapt to changes. The motivation behind this is sometimes questionable, with feminism shading into other views of society where certain groups of men have been demonized and blamed for the problems of society as a whole or for simply defending self-interest. One thing is clear. This is no longer the time for a war of words about which is the subordinate sex, but for a much more clear-headed look at what's really going on.

If anything gives a jolt to feminist certainties about the male oppressor, and invites us to look again at the changes affecting men, it is the growing evidence of male depression. In the early 1990s, statistics from the Samaritans revealed that in ten years male suicides had increased by 80 per cent, especially among young men. It was an extraordinary revelation, and not just because it highlighted what was already subjectively known, that those years had been a dispiriting time. What it also highlighted was a gender imbalance; female suicides actually decreased in the same period. Such evidence was hard to incorporate into a traditional feminist view of the world in which men always have the advantages and always come off better than women.

The only feminist spins which could be put on this were entirely malicious. Either it became a sick joke along the lines of, 'Good! At least men are now feeling the same way as women: bloody miserable.' Or it was a sign of men's greater weakness faced with difficult times. But spite apart, these statistics posed some uncomfortable questions. Were they evidence that pressures on men were now greater than those on women? And if so, why? Did it mean that men could actually be more vulnerable than women in difficult times, perhaps even the main victims of those times?

Of course, many commentators grabbed at common-sense explanations of this phenomenon. The higher incidence of male suicide didn't tell us anything about men and masculinity; it was a straightforward response to economic changes. Since the unemployment connected with the deepening recession of the late 1980s hit men harder than women, they said, it was hardly surprising that they should be disproportionately represented. Given that, traditionally, men's identity and self-esteem were so closely tied up with work, common sense suggests men are more likely to be affected by economic changes.

Announcing these statistics in November 1993, the chief executive of the Samaritans, Simon Armson, warned against making this simple causal link between unemployment and male suicide. After all, in the 1930s it was the bankrupts, formerly rich men, who committed suicide. Among the unemployed themselves, though suffering poverty and hardship far greater than anything experienced these days, there was no enormous increase in suicides. Instead, Armson included the issue of gender in his explanation, choosing to concentrate on the fact that the most significant increase in suicides was among young men, an increase which he attributed to the confusions of the new man – a theme eagerly seized on by the press. The new man, said Armson, 'is a confused young man and he is not quite sure how he is supposed to behave'. In particular, Armson blamed men's inability to communicate feelings and get help. 'Men find it more difficult to articulate their feelings of distress and prefer to bottle them up. Women find it easier to explain and put things in perspective' (quoted in the *Observer*, November 1993).

Obviously he was right to reject a direct link between worsening economic conditions and suicide. Indeed, it appeared that male suicide was actually highest during the period 1981–90 when unemployment rates were comparatively low. But Armson's interpretation may also have been an over-hasty dismissal of financial pressures and an over-idealization of 'feminine' survival techniques. In fact, research published by Mind, the mental health charity, at roughly the same time as the Samaritans' research in 1993, showed that unemployed men are three times more likely to kill themselves than men in work. This may not be a causal link but it is certainly significant, suggesting that unemployment feels particularly catastrophic when others around you are actually employed.

Armson is nevertheless right to highlight gender. However direct the link with unemployment is thought to be, the statistics make one thing clear, namely that depression and the risk of suicide are now greater among men. Yet bald statistics shed no light on what exactly these pressures on men were, why depression should be their response and why pressure affects men and women differently.

As we have seen in previous chapters, what was happening by the late 1980s and the early '90s was not just a loss of jobs but also changing work patterns which created a multitude of different pressures. The increase in male suicides happened just when these changes to the economy really began to be felt across almost all sectors of society. In previous times of economic recession, unemployment mainly hit the traditional working classes, working in direct production. This area was hit again in the 1980s. On previous occasions recession was experienced as 'bad times' involving lay-offs and closures, not something permanent. This time when coal and steel production went into decline, it was the end.

At the same time, the traditional pattern of employment among the middle classes or white-collar workers was also affected. Cutbacks in the state services meant redundancies in professions which had grown steadily since the 1960s. By the end of the 1980s, too, as the recession bit deeper, many companies were forced to shed employees. Smaller companies, which had proliferated under Thatcher, also folded. 'Flexibilization in all its forms – including down-sizing, part-time contracts, contracting out – also had dramatic effects in introducing insecurity amongst groups of people hitherto used to pursue a steady straightforward career' (Ray Pahl, *After Success*, 1994). Such insecurity felt, from the top down, would add to uncertainty about social roles in general.

These were local versions of what was happening globally. Professor John Gray, who describes globalization as 'the rapid spread of new technologies throughout the world', suggests that this social flux and its attendant insecurity, first felt in the early 1990s, are a permanent and inevitable consequence of such an economy: 'What globalisation does is not so much increase the number of jobs we have in a working life time. It continually wipes out entire occupations. Unceasing technical innovation has plunged the division of labour in society into a flux that will be with us from here on' (*False Dawn*, 1998).

Perhaps this is what has made recent economic changes feel far more unsettling than previous recessions. Subconsciously, at the very least, the absolute end of the traditional male career was beginning to be faced across all sectors of the community. Unskilled labourers faced an economy in which their role had been permanently shaken. White-collar workers faced the end of any sense of stable employment with one employer and steady progress up a career ladder. This endemic insecurity about working life has special difficulties for men, undermining as it does one of the unspoken assumptions that the role of breadwinner would always be open to men, whether they wanted it or not.

It is for this reason that the changes in western economies in the early 1990s had particular symbolic resonance. Few feel nostalgia for full-time jobs in industries such as coal and steel, but the demanding physical labour associated with such industries had in the past been a sort of benchmark of masculinity, a proof of men's toughness and endurance, a living embodiment of the sacrifices and hardships which supposedly justified masculine authority in society. Of course, this kind of labour was only ever performed by the poorest and least powerful members of society but the political and social power of middle-class men borrowed from this work. And as this work also symbolized the wealth of the country, even workers in those industries acquired a kind of status, however appalling their individual conditions. After the closure of these industries, the media were full of stories about role-reversal homes where depressed and unemployed men lethargically tended the children while their wives became the breadwinners. More important was the effect of these closures on the deeply-held, unexamined symbolism of sexual relationships. The sexual economy of the traditional labouring household had symbolic resonances for all of society. When assumptions about gender were shaken in that community it undermined a source of self-esteem from which all men, however distant from such work, benefited.

Individually, too, the changes affecting men's employment were rarely experienced as progress. Increased insecurity and a shift to flexible contracts and hours were highly problematic for those who, however unconsciously, had taken for granted that being the uninterrupted earner was at least an option. To lose that option felt more like a loss than slow progress to equality. Many men, especially in secure jobs, have long recognized the attractions of a more egalitarian household with a more open, affectionate relationship both with women and children, and more involvement in parenting. That is why feminism has always won amazing amounts of support from men. But such expectations are hardly relevant in a situation where insecurity, obstacles and restricted horizons are the order of the day. It is one thing planning for a more equitable role in the family by choice, quite another to experience unemployment, or unexpected insecurities, to have choices removed which undermine a whole sense of identity. 'Our sense of self', wrote Sean French in the *Guardian* (18 May 1998), 'went along with our social role, being a father . . . was also about being the supporter of the family, the person who went out and came back with rewards in the form of money and punishments in the form of your belt.'

In the early 1990s I interviewed many men about work and asked whether they considered that the pressures on them had significantly increased over the past ten years. Most agreed strongly. And all headed their lists of grievances with the general insecurity now pervading the workplace. Many felt that working relationships had become very unpleasant. They were forced to work obsessively, rarely felt their positions were secure and were often extremely anxious about implications for the family. One man, Michael, was in a situation typical of these changing economic realities and their pressures. His experiences and responses also seem typical of the complex interaction of economic and personal pressures which put men in the firing-line in the 1990s. The context of his stress was the new insecurity of the job market, but his ability, or inability, to deal with these stresses went much deeper. What he was really struggling with was loss of confidence and self-esteem in terms of what he offered as a man within the family.

When I interviewed him, Michael was in his early thirties, married with three young children. He had left a university lectureship in the mid-1980s to set up his own graphic design company on the strength of a large contract. By the late '80s, he had failed to win any other contracts of equal worth and the company was working on numerous smaller and short-term projects. When I spoke to him, he was suffering badly from depression and gave a particularly graphic account of his current working life:

> I work in a very competitive area where the loss of one project means that the whole business is under threat. When there is work, it has to be done under such tight deadlines and costings that most creative enjoyment is drained out of it. And between times the uncertainty and rejection is very difficult to live with. The kind of rejections I get now are so harsh; they really begin to undermine your belief in your own worth. I want to behave in a caring way at work but the industry I am in is anything but caring. It has become the worst kind of primitive capitalism. The best you can do is huddle together as a small team and provide some kind of support for one another.

Michael was upset by the harshness of his working environment, in particular the fact that he constantly had to expand and contract his workforce according to 'work flow'. Roughly translated, this meant constantly sacking and rehiring people. What distressed him even more was the effect of these stresses on him as a family man:

> There are many days when I would willingly chuck all this in and walk away. But I feel financially responsible for the

family. This is ridiculous on the face of it. My partner works and she is capable of earning a good living, although she chooses to work part-time at the moment. But I'm still driven by the fear that if I'm not bringing in money, our whole life will come crashing down in ruins. I feel panicky about not being able to provide.

It makes me so tense that I am certainly no fun at home. But the children have no means of understanding when I suddenly lash out at them. When I'm at home, I'm preoccupied by work. When I'm at work I worry about the family. I'm more and more certain that I would be well out of it all, if there was anywhere to go.

As Robert Bly put it rather more poetically in *Iron John* (1990): 'what the father brings home today is usually a touchy mood, springing from powerlessness and despair mingled with long standing shame and the numbness peculiar to those who hate their jobs.'

What this particular story illustrates is how distressed men can become about work pressures which might affect the family. There is a failure of imagination in Michael's worries about how family life could be lived in any satisfactory way if his work did fail. He worries about letting his family down, about his wife needing to work longer hours, and about jeopardizing things the family has come to take for granted; in short, about renegotiating gender roles without letting anyone down. These personal anxieties show that something deeper is happening in men's psyches. There has been a loss of confidence about what might be expected of them when the old job expectations have gone, and a difficulty about imagining a new role after the failure of the old ones.

These anxieties cannot be reduced to recession blues, nor to the feminist cliché of 'men's inability to share their feelings'. This interpretation of what has been happening to men has a crude Californian psychobabble superficiality. Andrew Samuels, a Jungian analyst who has written several books about men, suggests (interview with author, 1993) that the opposite may be true. He points out that, if anything, the past two decades have seen men 'opening up' more. Many men are now prepared to acknowledge problems and talk about their own behaviour.

> In theory, they are more able to admit their feelings now. It's not so taboo. In the past, depression would have been a 'feminine' reaction only open to women and 'effeminate' or weak men (such as artists). Now men are allowed to get depressed. That could be a good thing. A depressed state is not entirely negative. It can be a time for reassessment, withdrawal and attention to creative parts of the self which have been neglected. But you have to stay with depression for that to emerge.

From this perspective, Samuels has a different interpretation of the increase in suicides. He thinks men are currently unable to stay with that depression in a way which could be creative. Traditionally, men have been taught they have to act. And therapists tell us that if you act when you are depressed, it often means suicide. The increase in suicide may be the negative side of a positive shift. Men are halfway down the road to change. They can acknowledge depression but they cannot stay with it. Michael says he now frequently questions the point of living as he does, but adds: 'Once you start questioning yourself like this it becomes very scary. And there's not much point going on about it. I need to sort something out quickly.' This is a case in point; he can acknowledge the depression but is desperate for action.

But what precisely is it that is causing depression? After all, men's response to changing circumstances could be straightforward anger or even relief. Clinical perspectives illuminate what Michael's comments have already told us. Depression, therapists say, is closely associated with loss. If men are now experiencing more depression, it is not just that they are experiencing difficulties and changes but that they are experiencing loss. So what is it that men have actually lost?

In some quarters at least, men have not lost actual power.

As the feminist fundamentalists point out, in general they still earn more than women, they have more freedom in careers and certainly more freedom of movement. But, according to Samuels (in 'Analysis', Radio 4, March 1998), men are feeling a loss of status, of moral authority:

> There's been a one-sided busting of the male deal ... The male deal we signed up for both consciously and unconsciously was that if we turned away from softness, play, emotional connection – everything so-called feminine – and became the men we all know – the 'trad' man, then society would reward us with domination of women and children, material wealth, political prominence and a chance to define culture. Well, we did all that but the reward didn't come.

Samuels insists that men's perception of loss is just that – a perception. Male powers and privileges remain just about the same as they always were, that is, some men are very powerful and others much less so. What has changed is inside men, in what they do and how they relate to people and because they feel the old pay-off is not coming. 'It's all the hoohah around men's roles,' says Samuels, 'all the questions about, "is there a place for men and have women usurped or taken over or whatever?" All that has made men think, "Hey I'm not getting what I'm supposed to get."' In other words, it is a crisis of the psyche, of culture, of symbolism, of how men represent themselves to themselves.

To say that the loss is at the level of the symbolic and perceptual is not to downplay it. 'The crisis of masculinity is both real and deep-seated, and it cuts right across classes and age groups,' says Vic Seidler, lecturer in Social Theory at Goldsmiths College. 'The combination of large-scale unemployment and feminism has forced men to rethink how they've been brought up as men, both in the workplace and home. It's causing deep anxiety and uncertainty' (*Guardian*, May 1996). As much as any literal change in economic and social power, these changes in what masculinity means are affecting how gender relations will be lived.

Another man who I interviewed at the same time as Michael confirms the idea that the increase in male depression is connected as much with the shaking up of traditional male responses as with actual changes in male occupations. Tony, in his twenties, was working as a fitter when I spoke to him. His work felt highly insecure as the small company he worked for had already laid off several employees. But more than the insecurity of his work, Tony was worried about having too little status in his marriage. Two years ago, he married Sally who had a child by a previous relationship. Recently, they separated and Tony returned to his parents' home, describing himself as very depressed.

> I never felt convinced that Sally wanted me around. I think she'd got used to being on her own with Daniel. Before she met me, she always used to take hers and Daniel's washing to her mum's. She kept on doing that even when I moved in. I had to sort my own out. It sounds trivial but it was all part of her going on doing what suited her and not taking account of me. It was as if I didn't really belong. Her mother was set against me too. She's really down on men. Whenever we went round there, her mum had a group of her peculiar friends, all bitching about men and, of course, Sally joined in. When we got back, we really laid into each other – not fighting, but terrible arguments.

It would be easy to interpret Tony's complaint as that of the wounded male chauvinist, suffering from not having his washing done, but what he is really complaining of is the lack of intimacy implied by their separate arrangements. His depression seems much more connected with a failure to find a companionate relationship, rather than a desire to be the old-fashioned lord and master. It is an impression borne out by his views on his stepson: 'I'm really upset about losing Daniel. I took him swimming and to football every weekend. I wish Sally and I had managed to have a child; then maybe we would have been a proper family. I try to take my mind off it. I'm doing lots of overtime at work and playing a lot of football.'

Both Michael's and Tony's accounts are especially interesting in relation to Andrew Samuel's observations because they go to the heart of what he would consider another clue to the increase in male suicides. Tony is quick to deny physical violence, and Michael worries about his short temper with the children. 'The days when male aggression was accepted in an uncomplicated way are over,' says Samuels. 'That doesn't mean that the frequency of male violence has gone down. But it has got more complex. There are more "ifs" and "buts". If men bashed their wives around in the past, it wasn't a problem for themselves. Now it is.'

In a post-feminist culture, externally directed male aggression is much more problematic in relationships. This is not to say that it doesn't still happen but that both women *and* men feel much more resistant to this. It has become much more problematic to express moral authority uncritically through the power of physical violence. And if aggression cannot go outwards, it sometimes turns inwards. Therapists tell us that suicide is an act of violent aggression and, significantly, the real increase in male suicides has occurred among young men. It is this same group whose violent aggression also causes problems elsewhere.

This is a very different interpretation of the increase in male suicide and it requires that understanding goes a lot deeper than the favoured explanations of unemployment, 'male inarticulateness', 'loneliness', or fear of the sexual forwardness of the 'new woman'. It also challenges feminist claims that this is evidence of men clinging to the wreck of traditional male roles, unable to cope once women cease to mother and direct them; Mummy's Boys who won't be weaned. The real reasons for suicide go deeper. What's at stake is a new internalizing of criticisms of male behaviour and self-restraint, alongside aggression and anger which cannot be dealt with.

These suicide figures provide evidence not of men clinging to the old roles, but of men in the process of change. They are no longer confident about their old responses and are certainly seeking more from their relationships with women. But with the upheavals in working practices and their attendant psychic insecurities, the process can be painful. If men are oppressors, then they are vulnerable ones. This evidence of male vulnerability is not the same as the claims made by the likes of Fay Weldon and Melanie Phillips that men have become victims of a new matriarchy; it is more a recognition that the power and emotional certainties that went with the old patriarchy are on the move. Men have been forced into changes – in intimacy, in emotional responses, in working patterns and in the family. They often welcome these changes but change is not always easy. Economic and social upheavals mean that the old patterns of male employment, and the ready-made lifestyles that went with it, have gone. For many this involves real losses, not just of employment and security but of status, self-esteem and the old moral authority which men used to have just by being men.

MASCULINITY: FROM POTENCY TO ABSURDITY

The proposal that men have lost moral authority tends to provoke some of feminism's most bitter scorn. 'Did they ever have it?' some ask. 'Surely women always had the monopoly of that?' But I am not talking about the moral authority which fell to women in the past because they guarded private morality while men involved themselves in the public arena. I am talking about a more nebulous notion of authority, the authority of having more status, weight and gravitas by virtue of your sex, something which in the past belonged exclusively to men and which by definition required inferiority as its opposite.

In her novel, *A Thousand Acres* (1991), Jane Smiley gives us a portrait of exactly what male authority could entail. The father in the novel is a farmer who works non-stop for his family, but in return expects and commands absolute obedience. He takes his status as economic head of the household as entitlement to terrorize by threats or mood, even the moods brought about by drink. He flirts, cajoles and beats his three daughters who walk around him as if treading on glass. Each daughter negotiates his capricious flirtatiousness and his threats in different ways. And when he suddenly abdicates his position, like a latter-day King Lear, it is clear his daughters have all suffered and been damaged by the imposition of this arbitrary authority.

No wonder women have put up a fight against this authority. And if male despair is connected with a sense of loss, men are not imagining things. It is this unquestioned authority of masculinity which has gone, shaken by cultural changes which have undermined male certainties. These have as much to do with changes in attitude, in how social problems are defined, and in media representations, as they do with tangible economic and political changes. Because of this, they are easily dismissed: as we have seen in the previous chapters, feminists downplay them as ephemeral fashions which bear no relation to the lived (economic) reality of men and women. Yet these are the cultural forces which frame how individuals feel about their lives and how they make sense of society. It is hard to avoid the contemporary inference that masculinity no longer implies an automatic superiority but almost its opposite – difficulties, problems, inferiority.

Nowhere is this change in men's fortunes clearer than in how they are represented in advertising. In the 1970s, advertisements were the benchmark of women's oppression. By the 1990s – if adverts are to be believed – men are underneath. In feminism's early days, feminists branded as 'offensive' those adverts which showed women as inferior, either as brainless second-class citizens, or as 'sex objects' – temptresses and sexual adjuncts to men. What was exposed was the way in which femininity implied inferiority and no other aspect of society, it was said, made clearer the relative powerlessness of women.

Most people, however, uninterested in feminist politics, accepted these complaints. They could sympathize with women's objections to seeing themselves portrayed vacuously discussing the relative merits of washing powders or, scantily dressed, draped across the front of a motor car. They also understood that, if these were the principal images in circulation, they would reinforce or perhaps even create a general contempt for women in society.

'Sexual liberation' did not help matters either. Increased sexual explicitness brought its own problems. Women ceased to be just bimbos and hostesses but the new sexual openness was sometimes used to suggest women's collusion with predatory attitudes towards them. The Lovable bras campaign was typical. This showed a 'liberated' woman striding confidently along the street at night, apparently spurning a sexual advance. In a smaller frame on the same poster she was shown willingly undressing later, revealing that 'underneath they are all lovable'. Feminists claimed this was reinforcing an ideological justification of rape, that if a woman says no, she really means yes. Strip off her clothes to reveal the lovable woman underneath.

Such was feminism's concern about this contempt and hostility towards women that it spawned a whole industry of academic books and courses on the subject of advertising. These rarely questioned the portrayal of men, mainly because at that point it would have been hard to define any systematic treatment of men; they either featured as the 'norm', portrayed in a whole range of activities and types, or as the powerful counterpoint to women. It was women who were the 'defined' sex, confined to limited categories and powerless roles.

This all changed in the 1980s. First came images of strong independent career women, like Virginia Slims' cigarette adverts with their images of confident women and their feminist message, 'We've come a long way'. Then, more surprisingly, men began to be presented as hopeless and unappetising. In no time at all this became a new stereotype of 'girls on top' – women presented as glamorous, cool, competent and, in any exchange with men, the winners. By contrast, men's inadequacies had become a favourite topic. Men were now appearing in a far from favourable light. Ranging from dim and uncouth to pushy and insensitive, by the 1990s they had become the butt of advertising's humour.

The list of advertisements promoting this stereotype is very long indeed. In an advert for Kenco coffee a woman was shown humiliating the men around her, professionally and socially; a Shell ad showed men stupidly trying to clean parts of their car engines in the launderette; in a Norwich Union ad, a New Man sponged off his successful girlfriend; the advert for the Peugeot 106 showed a woman being harassed at work then returning home. When her partner asks if she has remembered to collect his dry cleaning she walks out. Nissan promoted its cars with an anxious-looking male intimidated by a dominatrix figure.

In 1993, Prudential Pensions was the subject of a complaint to the Advertising Standards Commission that it made men look dumb. The complaint was unusual but the message of the advert had become increasingly common. This one portrayed a man and woman sitting on a sofa expressing their hopes for the future. The woman is clearly ambitious and clever. She announces that she wants to buy a big yacht and travel around the world. The man is insensitive and slow on the uptake. 'We want to be together,' he announces, and sits there dimly while the woman registers contempt.

In the 1990s contempt for men became such a familiar part of advertising's rhetoric that few even stop to think about it. In a recent advert for Soft and Shine, the alleged qualities of the product were set against how men use the bathroom; men are dirty, uncouth, leaving toilet seats up, dropping towels on the floor and so on. There are assumptions about men here which, if applied to women, would seem highly problematic. To suggest that there is something disgusting about femaleness, as when the managers of Newcastle football team called the local women 'dogs' in 1998, would provoke outrage.

Other attitudes which have become unacceptable around women have become the norm around men. The 1998 Coca-Cola advert reversed the stereotype of woman as sex object, showing various female office workers and executives awaiting the arrival of the body beautiful, a handsome young man with Coca-Cola, becomingly sweaty. The women exchange glances indicating a shared fantasy of what they would like to do to him. Yet to represent a woman in the context of a group of predatory males would be unacceptable. Similarly, the Lee jeans advert which showed a woman's foot in a stiletto shoe resting on a man's naked bottom would have been widely condemned if applied to women. But apart from a brief flurry of media interest, no one really objected to the obvious connotations of sexual domination and humiliation. Indeed, sexual humiliation by women is now a standard part of advertising's rhetoric. In an advert for Highland Spring water a woman rejects a man because his bottle is too small, an act of symbolic castration.

Many women see this discourse around masculinity in advertising as an essentially humorous role reversal. 'This is the first time', said Rosie Boycott, now editor of the *Daily Express*, then editor of *GQ* magazine, 'that we've seen men made fun of. Men are being ridiculed. It's done with a lot of humour and is much better than the portrayal as helpless housewives that women have had to endure' (*Sunday Times*, April 1992). And unlike in the 1960s and '70s when feminists first attacked advertising, the audience is now far more sophisticated. No one really now thinks that adverts reflect reality in any simple way. Indeed, some might say that it is only because men are in fact the more powerful group that they are prepared to expose themselves as the butt of this kind of sexist humour; perhaps in so doing they create a false impression of women's power which then deflects from an understanding of the real injustices against women. At the very least, it is said, if women had to put up with offensive stereotypes for so long, surely it can do no harm for men to experience belittlement?

While adverts may not reflect reality directly, they do say something about social attitudes. The more sophisticated feminist analyses always recognized that adverts rather than reflecting reality in a straightforward way, often have a finger on the prevailing social pulse and recirculate or recast existing ideas. What the current adverts bear witness to is the idea that the traditional notions of masculinity are a joke. The old 'qualities' of masculinity – a narrow focus on life, domestic incompetence signalling a mind on higher things, emotional reserve and acts of endurance – have become absurdities, signs more of incompetence, insensitivity, lack of intelligence than of strength. Traditional masculinity has been rendered at best absurd and at worst somewhat menacing – a quality which needs to be taught a lesson, cut down to size by a dominatrix figure.

Advertisers clearly feel confident that this representation of the state of relations between the sexes is either how the majority perceive it to be or how the majority wish it to be. It is not difficult to see what they might be picking up on. From the humorous disparagement of men – an early amiable response to some of feminism's justified criticisms – through to more savage criticisms in the context of fears of social disintegration

91

in the early 1990s, hostility to men and masculinity has not been hard to find in the last two decades.

Feminism was, of course, the main force behind this shift of perspective. The assumption of masculinity as the superior point from which to judge all other behaviour was obviously a fundamental way in which women had internalized ideas of inferiority. How that masculinity was lived out in relation to women was also a problem: coercive sexuality, aggression, sometimes violence, control. So disparaging this masculine behaviour as morally and intellectually inferior was one vital element in feminism's strategy against the old male-dominated political and social order.

It is interesting that this assault on old assumptions about male authority immediately spread far wider than of feminism. The adverts I have just discussed are proof of this. Most of them were made by men and aimed not to please a small bunch of politically motivated feminists but to catch the mood of the times. Men have readily colluded in this denigration of their own sex; they describe each other as linguistically stunted and emotionally crippled. Nick Hornby has made a career as a writer out of portraying masculinity as a neurosis. Both *Fever Pitch* (1992) and *High Fidelity* (1995) are books about the absurdities of what was once taken to be normal male behaviour; in the former a passion for football, in the latter a man's obsession with his record collection. Both present conventional masculine obsessions as signs of emotional inadequacy. As Harry Enfield says on the cover of *High Fidelity*: 'a very funny and concise explanation of why we men are as we are. If you are male, you should read it and then make your partner read it, so they will no longer hate you but pity you instead.'

Enfield and Hornby are typical of the ways in which making fun of traditional masculinity has become *de rigueur* in media circles for the aspirant young male. 'Almost every young male writer and journalist writes in that self-mocking vein, examining elements of erstwhile masculinity with a bitter smile,' says Natasha Walter in *The New Feminism*. This is not entirely new. British humourists such as the Monty Python team poked fun at aspects of traditional masculinity, especially the upper-class masculinity implicit in upholding establishment values. And contemporary comedians like Ben Elton and Jo Brand, although inspired by feminism, draw on elements from that other tradition too. Yet their humour has a contemporary quality, often expressing hostility and contempt as much as good-humoured teasing. As Jo Brand recently quipped about how stupid it was to make racist jokes, 'That would be like saying all men are bastards. Er . . .' And this humour seems to appeal to a very wide audience.

In *Slow Motion* (re-issued 1997), feminist author Lynn Segal insists that, alongside all this critiquing of masculine absurdities, there has been a simultaneous reassertion of traditional masculinity. Many contemporary films, television programmes and especially men's magazines seem to celebrate a regressive form of unreconstructed masculinity: 'There are many ways of escaping from or else resisting change which include buying the *Sunday Sport, Loaded, Men Only*, generally behaving badly or laddishly.' Yet even the phenomena described by Segal betray men as having internalized the critique of masculinity as much as they are repudiating it. Natasha Walter describes the TV series *Men Behaving Badly* as 'articulating the loss of masculinity, not its power, by giving us laddishness as a fragile pose'.

Andrew Samuels goes further. He thinks that men's ideas about themselves have been rendered 'very much more complex and multi-layered by feminism'. So laddishness may well be a 'parodic' assertion of masculinity, found at all levels of society not just among middle-class men who have been directly influenced by feminism. 'This sort of parody of masculinity has actually trickled down to a very great extent so that lots and lots of different groups of men are able to get self-reflexive . . . stand outside themselves doing the behaviour that they do. A lot of young people – boys, even – know quite a lot about playing at being males' ('Analysis', Radio 4).

Parodic self-reflexivity is not exactly the same as loss of moral authority but they are connected. Parody and irony spring from not being able to inhabit old forms of behaviour without some distance. That's because male behaviour has been rendered problematic. Once attributes of masculinity were taken for granted as the position from which to judge all characteristics which deviated from this (especially so-called feminine attributes). But the media reflect a culture where the once desirable attributes of masculinity now seem absurd, fair game for humour and sometimes disgust. On the cultural stage the message is clear: men have fallen from grace. Masculinity is no longer a position from which to judge others but a puzzling condition in its own right.

Parody, self-reflexivity, the end of certainties. These terms evoke post-modernism, with its ideas of play, pastiche and performance, conjuring up visions of a world where individuals no longer feel destined by their biology to live out old fixed gender stereotypes. It could mean than both genders are at last free to stand back and choose how to express themselves. From this perspective, knocking men off the perch of their unearned authority looks an entirely positive development for both women *and* men. This is what happens when the old deal around sex roles finally breaks and it won't be long before men, just as much as women, recognize how little that deal offered them anyway. 'It is a bad time to be a man, compared with the supremacy which men have enjoyed in the past,' says sociologist John MacInnes in *The End of Masculinity* (1998), adding, 'and this is a thoroughly good thing.'

Genial masochism like this is what is expected of a good liberal when refuting the idea of a male crisis. Men's old privileges have gone; it is bound to hurt but it is necessary medicine; no fair-minded person should be sorry to see unearned authority go. Anyway, busting up the old male certainties has opened up not just uncertainties but also possibilities and freedoms. Men can now invent themselves, as women did at the birth of feminism, in all their roles as fathers, husbands, lovers, workers.

Certainly some men seem to have responded to such freedoms. It is impossible now to go shopping, to pick up a magazine or to watch television or films without finding some instance of men reflecting on their masculine identity. There are men's fashions, men's health issues, men's self-improvement products or courses. Studies of history such as Richard Phillips's *Mapping, Men and Empire* (1997) and Kim Townsend's *Manhood at Harvard* (1997) show that men are no longer leaving themselves out of the narrative but recognizing that masculinity was a construct which constrained men of previous generations even while giving them advantages.

Men's self-consciousness about being men is at such a pitch that it must be compared with women's self-consciousness when feminism first emerged. Typically, International Women's Day in 1996 was celebrated in the British media with an unprecedented amount of attention paid to *men*. On television there was a new series, *The History of Masculinity*, a series on the hidden problems of men's health, an Open Door programme about 'It's a bad time to be a man', and a polemical documentary by journalist Tony Parsons about what feminism has done to men. This was the same week in which the *Daily Mail* ran its week-long investigation into 'The Redundant Male'.

Women's events organized for that week were the same old events that feminists have been organizing for years. The only difference from feminism's early days was that, in keeping with the decline of the movement, the events have been on an ever-declining scale, such as women's art shows, advertised locally or in the small circulation women's magazine *Everywoman*. This difference between the public profile of the sexes in the week supposed to celebrate women's achievement and to promote their further gains sums up what had happened around the subjects of 'women' and 'men'. Men have come under scrutiny as never before, whereas the popular consideration of women has run out of steam. In feminism's heyday, everyone had agreed that women were 'the dark continent' but now men have become 'the final frontier'.

This change struck me with particular force. In the early 1980s I published an article ('Linguistic, Social and Sexual Relations') with a colleague, Maria Black, which argued against the then contemporary feminist truth that women were marginalized because they were absent or excluded from language. On the contrary, we argued, it was men who were often absent in discourses. Women were relentlessly defined *as* women whereas men need not even recognize themselves as men, only as people or humans. We argued that feminism had come into existence because, however different individual women's experiences, it was almost impossible to escape at some point being defined by the prevailing language and ideology as women. Under the somewhat prescient heading 'Ungendered Men, Endangered Species', we wrote: 'There is a discourse available to men which allows them to represent themselves as people, humanity, mankind. This discourse, by its very existence, excludes and marginalises women by making women *the* sex ... Men are sustained at the centre of the stage precisely because they can be "people" and not represent their masculinity to themselves.' We added rather pompously: 'Men can never be displaced from the centre until they can be forced to recognise themselves as men and take responsibility for this.'

The idea that ungendered man was an endangered species was obviously right. If asked to single out one dramatic cultural change over the 1980s and '90s, the change in male self-consciousness would have to be a leading contender. Most is just part of the wider culture – in films, on television and in magazines, especially those marketed to men – not confined to discussion of a 'male crisis'. Best-selling men's magazines now outsell women's magazines, an unthinkable situation in the days when men were only addressed via their hobbies. And there's a steady stream of books about men, whose titles say it all: *Fire in the Belly – On Being a Man*; *The Way Men Think*; *Shadow of the Stone Heart*; *Men and the Water of Life*; *Masculinity and Psychoanalysis*; *A Man's World*. I could go on. Suffice it to say that this is a boom area. As Neil Spencer put it in the *Observer* (17 December 1995), 'being a bloke it seems is big business', adding, 'business as usual some women might say'.

Spencer's joke correctly anticipates how many feminists have reacted to all this attention paid to men. When a few years ago I proposed a talk on the 'crisis of masculinity' for a Women's Studies course, the course organizer accused me of falling for 'Men's Movement propaganda'. 'Men already have too much attention in all walks of life,' she said. 'Why should we allow them in to colonize even those areas which women have made their own?' Such resistance is perhaps unsurprising. If women like this acknowledged the crisis of masculinity as a real crisis, not just a media fantasy, it would expose the theoretical inadequacies in their notions of male power and female subordination.

At the same time it was also an extraordinary reaction. How could any contemporary study of gender relations ignore the fact that, in the public domain at least, what was happening to men seemed more urgent than what was happening to women? To dismiss this as the Women's Studies lecturer did as imperialism disguised as harmless navel-gazing is facile. Self-consciousness about identity and roles is a genuine response to changing economic and social reality, and just because the subject is man does not make it masculinist. Frank Mort, writing about the emergence of men's fashion styles in *Cultures of Consumption* (1996), points out that 'throughout the eighties the shifting nature of men's lives, their behaviours, fears and anxieties were scrutinised with a new intensity'. Men were specifically targeted as the new consumers in expanding fashion, leisure and self-improvement industries, men were incited to spend money on themselves in entirely new ways. But, he adds, 'it is no accident that all this occurred at precisely the moment when feminism was defining men as an object of political and intellectual concern'.

This makes feminism's hostility to any male self-consciousness particularly ironic. Feminism's focus was on the visibly objectionable aspects of male behaviour: paternalism, domestic violence, sexist attitudes and actual sexual assault. But other more nebulous aspects of masculinity were sucked into the same process. Feminism caused men to become self-conscious about their masculinity, initially in the context of being challenged for their inappropriate behaviour towards women, then, in the context of increasing insecurities in the 1990s, asking themselves what appropriate behaviour might be.

Indeed, probably the key aspect of feminism's success is this displacement of men from that position of neutral authority, the ungendered space, against which women as gendered subjects were always measured. Men can now be aware of themselves in a similar way, as having roles, as being constructed by discourses of masculinity in the same way that women became aware of how they had been positioned and restricted by discourses of femininity. Once you become aware of men as categories, history ceases to be a transparent discourse in which women are a problem, either absent or overly controlled. So it is not surprising to find many fascinating histories of masculinity beginning to appear. The best of these interrogate the production of the masculine as the flip-side of the production of the feminine, so that we are now beginning to get a fuller picture of the workings of power, in particular how certain models of heterosexual masculinity structured and oppressed everything which deviated from them. These studies no longer talk of 'masculinity' but only 'masculinities', the different places ascribed to men by different ideologies and social forces.

In many ways, this new consciousness among men about the need to understand where they are speaking from is an entirely positive development for gender relations. The old positions of power from which men spoke are now contested. Men cannot easily inhabit their old paternalistic positions. They cannot, for example, assume automatic leadership in business and in politics. This does not mean that men do not still occupy those positions but they do so in a more complex way. It is no accident that both Bill Clinton and Tony Blair have very strong, powerful wives and make much of them. In modern, democratic post-feminist countries an old-fashioned potent male leader – not neutralized by a strong female presence – is becoming increasingly problematic. White men speaking from those unreconstructed positions of power are likely to evoke discomfort and reaction because they would be drawing on notions of male leadership from the old disputed masculinities – aggressivity and dominance – unacceptable to many now.

Tony Blair has an assertive, in many ways old-fashioned, masculine stance, yet this is countered by the image of his wife.

99

Similarly, Hillary Clinton has been absolutely central in guaranteeing that Bill Clinton's presidency was seen as progressive.
The question of whether the sex scandals surrounding Bill Clinton would be catastrophic was seen to reside in how Hillary
Clinton would react, and, through her, American women in
general. In other words, it was clear that his behaviour could
not be excused in old-fashioned terms of powerful men being
entitled to abuse powerless women, but it could be excused if
American women decided it was 'modern'. In short, women
have become crucial in how male politicians now negotiate
their potency.

When things are going well, the new potency which women
have and the new ways of relating to each other are experienced
as enriching for both sexes. Men who expect equal and democratic relationships with women, especially if they have not been
in any way threatened or disadvantaged by social and economic
changes, welcome these developments. Young men now are far
less rigid about social roles. They do not necessarily expect to
be defined by their job; many are happy to swap roles with
their partners, staying at home to look after the children, feeling neither ashamed nor emasculated. The school gates often
have as many men as women waiting at them. Gay activists, too,
have welcomed all this; the feminist challenge to masculine
certainties made life very much easier for those who felt
excluded or oppressed by those rigid certainties about how
men should behave. In the 1990s there has been no rigidity of
fashion; there have been plural identities for men to adopt and
many different sexual styles.

Yet there are more complex aspects to these changes. Men
in more vulnerable circumstances can experience this self-
reflexivity as part of their problems. These would be men who
have experienced bitter divorces in which their wives appear
to have gained more; men who have lost jobs while the women
around them have flourished; and men raised with traditional
views of masculinity and femininity who feel threatened by the
need to question what they could previously take for granted.
The old certainties and positions from which to act are no

longer available in quite the same way and for some the compensations seem minimal. Feminists have made this particularly
difficult by claiming men deserve whatever discomfort they are
now feeling. It is not just that these men are no longer gods,
they feel like devils.

The loss of masculine authority has not been a simple process
of challenging masculine certainties, introducing welcome
doubt and self-reflexivity. As all the adverts discussed in the
previous chapter show, and the following chapter will elaborate,
it is not just that men have lost moral authority, it is also that
women appear to have acquired it. It is this shift, and how
the sexes are negotiating it, that is causing some of the most
rancorous exchanges about sex and feminism. So in the following chapters I am going to examine more closely what exactly
this shift has been and how various groups have negotiated it.
In particular, I am going to be looking at how this moral authority has shifted from men to women, how various groups have
responded to this, and how it has affected the crucial social
issues of our times: parenting, boys, and sexual relationships.

Nothing demonstrates the shift in the status of the sexes more clearly than ideas about heroism. There have been dramatic changes in those characteristics which our society designates as the most desirable or ideal, and this has clear implications for how each sex will feel about life and work.

Superficially it looks as if old-fashioned male heroism is still the order of the day. Tabloid newspapers are filled with feats of endurance, strength and bravery: the selfless heroes of the rescue services, the policemen who attend bombings, the head-master who died protecting his pupils. This looks much like the old heroism requiring the repression of physical and emotional needs in the service of others – country, family, friends – and the heroes are usually men. Indeed, when it comes to women exhibiting endurance, courage and strength, the media have been decidedly ambivalent. Fleur Hargreaves, one of Britain's first female firefighters, was a pretty, young, single woman who lost her life in a fire. The press treated her as heroic. But when Alison Hargreaves died climbing K2 the response was much more punitive. As a mother she had no right to take risks with a life on which others depended, especially when she was pursuing her own ambitions and pleasures, not saving other lives. So women only enter this preserve as proto-men, if they are young, single and tough.

Even though the tabloids continue to search for the mascu-line 'heroes', in the wider culture most people just laugh at the idea of traditional male heroism. Even those who get label-led heroes seem dismissive of those old roles. Typically, a British policeman, designated by the tabloids as the hero of the 1996

Docklands' bombing politely declined the position. 'I've done nothing heroic,' he said, 'nothing special. I'm just the one who made the checks on the vehicle and who has a very scratched face.' Philip Lawrence, the headmaster who was stabbed to death when he intervened to protect a pupil, was celebrated by his son at his memorial service as a gentle father not a warrior hero.

A more accurate vignette of how both sexes relate to this heroism in the 1990s is given in the most recent television series of *Superman*. The costume is the same, but Superman himself isn't quite what he used to be. In all previous versions, Superman's manly heroic feats – his timely transmogrifications from human to superhuman in order to save the world – were the real focus of the story. But now saving the world is merely a backdrop to a much more human struggle: the relationship between Clark Kent and Lois Lane.

Heroism in the '90s Superman is presented as a sort of workaholism which almost spoils the human relationship between Clark Kent and Lois Lane. She constantly hankers after Superman, not entirely seduced by the all too human and vulnerable Clark Kent. In turn, he can only convincingly make love as Superman. Saving the world is secondary to the really heroic struggle of whether Clark Kent can be brave enough to own up to his feelings, winning over Lois without the props of his Superman persona. For Lois the issue is whether he can be desired without his heroic attributes. The themes are revealing; male heroism is an absurd residual neurosis provoking ambivalent feelings and unwanted backward-looking structures of desire in both men and women.

Heroism used to be a male certainty, something expected and desired in men. But this kind of risk-taking, strength-based, protective male heroism became anachronistic some time ago. This is partly because, with the death of heavy industrial labour, current male working practices have little call for heroic acts of endurance and strength. Militarism, where heroic values might have a natural place, has since the 1960s been derided rather than glorified. Above all, feminism made heroism seem at best faintly ludicrous, at worst potentially threatening. From the position of a woman threatened by arbitrary power, strength and endurance could look like control and oppression. So what were once considered virtues (heroism, courage, indepen-dence, strength, rationality, will, backbone, virility) became masculine vices (abuse, destructive aggression, coldness, emo-tional inarticulateness, detachment, inability to communicate, to empathize and so on). They are the source now not of reverence but humour, sometimes even of contempt or fear.

When traditional risk-taking heroism was problematized there was a shift to stress-bearing heroism, a new heroism about coping with the difficulties of life. This is an area where women have always performed well and feminists, who know a thing or two about stress, were quick to capitalise. In the 1970s the feminist project of self-discovery – 'liberation' from repressive marriages or the self-denial of the traditional family – acquired, at least in many women's eyes, the status of an epic struggle. This was the theme of Marilyn French's era-defining novel, *The Women's Room*. The heroine's own struggle away from the repression of traditional female roles to a new freedom of self-expression was fundamental to perceptions of what feminism was about.

Yet it was the changes in women's employment patterns which really boosted their candidacy for this new kind of hero-ism. Combining work and family, especially if it was not just for self-advancement but to better the cause of all women, became *the* heroic project of the 1980s. Men's churlishness and lack of support only made women look better. The more women had to do-it-all to have-it-all, the more heroic their labours. Popular culture even gave a label to this female hero-ism; the 1980s, we were constantly reminded, was the decade of superwoman. Adverts showed her power-suited, kissing her house-husband goodbye, or returning from work to assume control over a house full of male incompetents.

The image of the power-dressed executive, briefcase in one hand, baby in the other, was never exactly a feminist ideal – feminists were always much too ambivalent about success in a capitalist system – but they certainly unintentionally played a part in making it the desirable image of the decade. For it was feminism which insisted that women should work, and that, if they wanted to, mothers should continue to work. They also persuaded women that, by doing so, they would be advancing women's lot in general. It was feminism which made working mothers feel like pioneers of a new, modern identity for women. Feminism rendered the ambitions of modern women magnificent, and gave women's attempts to be working mothers, to continue their careers, or even reach great personal career heights, a moral and ethical purpose. They were doing it on behalf of all women and there was glory to be had just by being different from what had gone before.

The economic and social changes which have so shaken men have only enhanced women's status. Not only could women enter all sorts of jobs previously closed to them – and experience a pioneering pleasure while so doing – but they became increasingly popular as employees at a time of increased casualization and part-time employment. Feminism also helped raise the prestige of mothering in general; instead of being an invisible natural activity, feminists demanded it should be recognized as work. So combining work and motherhood, although hard, gives added glory. It gave all women a tremendous sense of purpose and dynamism. 'Women', says Faludi, 'have completely overhauled their notion of what it means to be female, what their role and identity is in society. And even in the darkest hour that's not only a great comfort but it gives one a great sense of mission and meaning in life' (quoted in Susan Mitchell, *Icons, Saints and Divas*, 1997).

Feminism was never fashionable. Tabloids rarely missed an opportunity to represent all feminists as extremists, poking fun at boiler-suited lesbians. Successful women also tediously repeated the mantra of 'I'm not a feminist but . . .' Yet those who actually rejected feminism's project and argued for old-fashioned femininity seemed utterly anachronistic and irrelevant. So even though they distanced themselves from feminism, ordinary women and celebrities alike quite simply wanted a part of the female heroism which feminism had made synonymous with modern womanhood. This extended to any-thing women could do to redefine their previous lives, including sexual behaviour or appearance, but it particularly affected com-bining motherhood and work. It became *de rigueur* for celebrities to parade the fact that they too fulfilled the necessary criteria, parading their expanding families.

Needless to say, the popular and widely accepted version of female heroism has become a very different entity from its feminist original. Consumerism recast it as the woman who could combine work and home while retaining her traditional feminine allure. Away from feminism, the emphasis was on the triumph of women who maintain their looks and figures, ensuring that having children did not spell the end of a social or sexual life. So the media heroines were those who didn't just work but worked on themselves, retaining the perfect body, clothes and health in the face of the transformations wrought by age and childbirth. Celebrities like Demi Moore and Paula Yates appropriated the heroic language to talk of their battles to maintain their figures and their sex lives despite motherhood.

The fact that female heroics have displaced the traditional male heroics is not the same as saying that only women can be heroes now. Far from it. But it does have a real effect on women, and on men and boys too. No wonder the self-esteem of girls is said to be very much greater than that of boys at present and is affecting their academic performance. It's not difficult to understand why. Just as all men benefited in self-esteem because some of their gender exhibited the idealized qualities, all women benefit because some of their gender carry the heroic attributes of the age. Is there any incentive for boys to want to join the world of men? asks Adrian Mourby, pondering on how the supercompetence of his wife around the home must appear to their son. 'Certainly if there isn't then I can understand the current phase of underachievement in schoolboys. Who wants to grow up to be a superannuated parent, baffled by new tech-nology, stranded by changing social mores and eclipsed by Superwoman?' (*Guardian*, 7 January 1998).

Some women, of course, were keen to introduce a degree of realism into this heroic project. Shirley Conran, the title of whose book, *Superwoman*, became shorthand for 1980s heroism, denounced it soon afterwards as oppressive to women. She was aware that many career women did not want to be lionized; many wanted the true costs and difficulties to be known, something often glossed over in the media's simplistic picture of the 'have-it-all' generation. Many women pointed out that having it all did, of course, include having the nervous breakdown.

Women, arguing for a dose of reality, weren't the only critics of this new female heroism. In many different cultural areas, there were spirited attempts to reinvent male heroes in this new garb. Many contemporary male icons lay claim to the old notions of working-class male heroism, like the spectacle of celebrities and pop stars describing their lives in terms of gruelling or punishing schedules. They talk of their work in Stakhanovite terms, each competing with the other for the most pressurized life, appropriating somewhat obscenely to themselves the heroism of hard physical labour. Typically, Liam Gallagher bowed out of an American concert tour in 1996, describing the pressures of the tour as too great when his heart was really in England, house-hunting with his new partner Patsy Kensit. Absurdly, the worlds of pop music and the media ape the exhausting labours of working-class men in earlier eras.

This nostalgia for the old male hero crops up all over. One ideal for the male body, fashioned by work-outs in the gym, is like a bizarre parody of the working-class male hero. Only this time the heroic body has been produced by leisure not labour. These bodies, muscular and taut, also echo the male heroes of children's cartoons, certainly an area of culture where male heroism remains alive and well. In cartoons such as *Thundercats* and *Power Rangers*, girls may now be acknowledged but the focus is invariably the male-dominated gang, committed to archaic beliefs about heroism and devoted to the cult of fighting.

Another spirited defence of male heroism came from a biologist writing a book on the struggle between 'warrior' sperm to fertilize a woman's egg. In *Sperm Wars*, published early in 1996,

Dr Robin Baker described the battles of the ejaculate in Homeric terms. The sperm were 'magnificent, sleek and athletic'. Battles apparently are fought between the sperm belonging to different men after a woman deliberately sleeps with several different men in order to maximize her chance of getting the best sperm. These battalions of sperm have different divisions, such as foot soldiers. Presumably all this is meant to prove that the male warrior lives on, at least inside the male body if not in his social being.

Some of the attempts to restore male heroism are more explicit, more political. For Robert Bly, guru of the American Men's Movement, the loss of heroism is critical in the malaise of modern men. In *Iron John* (1990) he claims that he is constantly encountering 'emasculated men' who are always charming, always in support of feminism but essentially unhappy. He diagnoses the condition of contemporary men as 'soft', caused by men being cut off from positive male energy. This is the energy embodied in the quintessential hero of the Iron John myth which Bly describes as a journey of 'resolve', 'decisiveness' and 'quickness'. He exhorts men to get in touch with these attributes of masculinity by owning their instinctive side, the infamous hairy man within for which he has been so mocked. Heroism is vital in this journey to a separate, strong male identity: 'American man today needs a sword to cut his adult soul away from his mother-bound soul.'

Feminists are quick to describe this as evidence of a woman-hating male supremacy that will not be shaken from its positions of authority. These are manifestations of nostalgia, reminders of men's real power when under threat from social changes. But who is really feeling this nostalgia for the old male hero? For every one man expressing such nostalgia, a dozen women can be found being even more scathing than the men about the problem of men who have become insipid by abandoning traditional masculine values. Robert Bly looks mild beside some of the women writers mourning the loss of masculine hardness. Jo-Ann Goodwin, writing in the *Observer* (13 February 1993), describes 'new men' as the 'toxic waste' of feminism: 'The worst thing of it is these men are so unappealing, so unaesthetic, so unsexy . . . He's so busy trying to be supportive he's probably forgotten what an erection is for.'

More humorously, Sue Limb makes the same point (*Guardian*, 9 January 1998), ruing the passing of the days when you could 'get a man in' to do jobs around the house: 'Nobody had low sperm count in those days . . . The men in one's life have turned to putty. Although they have forgotten what putty is . . . They're conditioning their pony tails. They're changing the nappies. They're whipping up coulis. They're going on courses in bonding and self-fulfilment.' 'The idea of being married to a man who is as touchy-feely as an octopus, fills me with horror,' adds Juliette Mead in the *Daily Mail* (17 September 1997), commenting on the rise of the 'feminine' man. 'Frankly, I'll take Action Man over Knitting Ken any day.'

But all this noise about heroism and traditional masculine virtues, whether coming from women or men, is just that: noise. The contemporary male hero remains, like Christopher Reeve, a superman in a wheelchair, what Jungians would doubtless call 'a wounded hero'. The majority of men in the West are quite simply not interested in restoring the mantle of heroism. The Men's Movement remains a seriously minority movement in the UK; no one wants to be associated with 'the men who moan too much'. It was extremely revealing that so many men laughed at Peugeot's 1996 advert. Having been leaders in the field of emasculating-women adverts, Peugeot suddenly changed tack, attempting to revive images of male heroism to sell their cars. Set to the music of 'Search For The Hero Inside Of You', the advert was a series of traditional images of heroic acts, like rescuing a little girl from in front of a truck. Most of the images were out-of-date clichés, but one might have rung a bell, when the otherwise heroic man faints at the sight of his newborn baby. This is not the old cliché of the tough man who faints at the sight of blood; now men faint because of the awesome responsibility. It takes a real hero to recognize what it means to be a father.

There's a clue here to what has been happening. Male heroes

have not disappeared; they've changed. Increasingly, the only convincing contemporary representation of heroism is that of an inner struggle towards greater awareness and deeper relationships; that is, a struggle towards a more 'feminine' position. This is one of feminism's most important legacies. It gave enormous significance to women's struggle to transform themselves, and cope with complex demands from different areas of their lives. And now men want to be part of this project. In this respect the 1990s television *Superman* is closely in touch with the contemporary ethos. Tongue-in-cheek though the whole programme may be, its location of heroism in the struggle of Superman to achieve a deep relationship with a woman is an accurate parable of the relationships between the sexes at this time. Both sexes are troubled by a continuing desire for male potency, but the only true heroism available to men now is an inner struggle from the repression which previously propped up and made possible acts of physical courage and heroism, to an ability to express human and tender emotions.

The really heroic struggle is now about facing inner obstacles, owning up to emotions in order to become a less repressed person. This is one of the reasons why fatherhood has become a central theme of contemporary fiction and cinema. Especially in Hollywood, the struggle of the father to connect to his child is the ultimate symbol of the struggle men have to become more authentic people. *Fly Away Home* (1996) is a typical film of the times. As is so often the case in these films, the mother is dead (in some films she has abandoned the home). The central dilemma is whether or not the father can emerge from his protective male cocoon (work or repression) and connect with his lonely child. The theme is duplicated in numerous other areas: Nick Hornby's *About a Boy* (1998) contains identical preoccupations – a man making an emotional journey to self-knowledge through friendship with a young boy.

In the contemporary versions of masculinity on offer, risk-taking heroism is anachronistic, and stress-bearing heroism somewhat unreliable. There is always the danger that the latter might be exposed as completely vacuous. But the bravery of facing the old repressions, the old hindrances of the traditional male, in order to become a more sensitive being resonates with modern preoccupations. This is a heroism which appears to have value and purpose, a heroism of the inner moral life not of the external body. Indeed, even Robert Bly's book *Iron John*, which appears to be all about restoring real male heroism, turns out to be no more than an inner journey. After all the talk of swords and journeys and trials, the real process is an emotional ordeal, from a soft mother-bound state to a separate, strong, resolute male being. He writes: 'This process of reviving the inner warriors goes on for years, and it is associated with the change from copper to iron. Each of us needs to imagine how to bring the interior warriors back to life, and it is not physical work so much as imaginative work.' Heroism is an inner moral struggle rather than any external act.

Traditionally, emotional work towards the transformation of the self has been the preserve of women. In the 1960s and '70s, it was women who pioneered a struggle from one state – repressed and weighted down by the past – to a new state, the modern woman. Owning up to difficult emotions and transcending them was the path to this new state. There can be little doubt that Princess Diana exerted such a pull on the public imagination and not just the unusual and potent combination of glamour, royalty and compassion; it was also because of a very visible inner journey, from stifling within a conventional marriage, through a painful divorce, to a search for a sense of purpose away from a man and a companionate marriage. In this Diana could be represented as embodying what, through the legacy of feminism, is the heroic journey of our era. Although she lived out this journey long after Marilyn French made it the theme of her era-defining novel, *The Women's Room*, public empathy for Diana showed that this voyage was no longer a marginal hope of a minority group but central to women in a post-feminist culture.

The irony of Diana's death is that she has left behind a situation going to the heart of the new state of sexual politics. Charles is a most improbable character to fulfil the part of

Hollywood hero, but he has been handed a Hollywood narrative *par excellence.* A man burdened by repressions, tradition and lack of feeling is left on his own with two sons with the challenge of relating to them as the more humane, feminine Diana could. The desire to cast him in this narrative is already much in evidence. Nothing in his behaviour or his stance has changed, yet the tabloids are full of 'how Charles has become a more caring individual'.

It is easy to be irritated by much of this. And some of the men crowding in on this terrain can be very irritating indeed. Some talk in quasi-Arthurian terms of men's transformation into deeper and more rounded human beings, appropriating feminism's discourse on the pressures of work and family but grafting on the old images of male heroism to make it so much more powerful than the female version. Jack O' Sullivan, of the *Independent,* for instance, writes and talks as if this is an entirely male discovery, as if women have not thought about conflicts between work and emotional life, between parenting and public objectives, as if women and feminists have had no hand in the transformations which our society has already undergone. And when even tucking the children up in bed acquires the symbolism of dragon-slaying, it is hard not to draw the conclusion that men are so desperate to hang on to male heroism that they are willing to inhabit a female terrain.

This is a feminine project, however, not a female one and feminists are wrong if they imagine men's presence in this area is dispossessing women from something exclusive. Some men do seem to be bringing with them an old-fashioned male potency as they move on to this terrain – if nothing else the potency of demanding and getting other men's attention much more readily than women can. Also, if Hollywood films are anything to go by, there is a subliminal desire to remove women altogether, as revealed by the persistent theme of single fathers and absent mothers. But men's desire to perform well on this terrain also reflects a positive change for a society which wants equality. Knocked off the pedestal of being the judge and jury of all those who deviated from their standards, men have become those who must make the journey of personal transformation. Men have recognized what was so important in the founding moments of feminism – that there is work to do on identity and that it is difficult. They also know that unless they do it, they will not keep pace with the revolution begun by women.

It would be pleasing to report that women, confronted with the reversals of male fortune, have been consistently magnanimous and that they too have owned up to uncertainty about their future roles. However, some women seem to think that the downfall of the old masculine prestige is an opportunity for triumphalism about the rise of a new feminine one, and feminism has actively aided them. It is often feminists who hint that the shift in moral authority is not just from masculine to feminine but from men to women.

The assumption that women are the superior sex who should be supported in all efforts to impose feminine values can currently be heard everywhere. It is a commonplace of the late twentieth century that women really are the superior sex; that there would be no more war or corruption if more women were in politics (and this after Margaret Thatcher!); that women make better bosses, 'because they are prepared to put in extra effort and their supportive nature fits well with the modern workplace' (Survey quoted in the *Daily Mail*, 17 September 1997); that crime is a male problem; that women's expression of their sexuality is never harmful, and so on. In March 1998 a report in the science magazine *Focus* was widely cited in the tabloids. 'Women *will* take over the world', it said. 'Females are both psychologically and physically stronger ... They are smarter, more sociable and kinder to themselves than boys and when they grow up, they get further along the career ladder, earn more and manage their families better. The findings suggest that the world could soon be under the control of some remarkably superior beings' (*Daily Mail*, 17 March 1998).

You would expect to find sweeping generalizations about men and women – with the emphasis on men's vices and women's virtues – among certain types of feminists. Sexism, the systematic disparagement of women by men, has been the main way in which economic and social injustices against women are justified, so a vengeful repudiation and reversal might seem inevitable. Radical feminists certainly never missed a chance to expose male behaviour as morally and intellectually inferior. Yet these feminists, with their emphasis on the essential differences between men and women and their overt antagonism to male behaviour, were always loathed by the media, and regularly characterized as 'lesbian man-haters'. So it is especially surprising to see that contemptuous hostility towards masculinity and its concomitant idealization of women are much more general phenomena, part of the wider culture.

This glorification of female superiority spread with amazing rapidity from radical feminism into the mainstream media; in the 1980s it was hard to find a women's magazine which did not cultivate this angle on men in one or another article. Susan Faludi claims that in the 1980s American magazines and newspapers were bristling with anti-feminism; she cited as evidence numerous articles about high-flying career women who gave up jobs to become full-time mothers, or women who left getting pregnant so late that they ceased to be fertile. In fact, those themes were insubstantial by comparison with the endless outpourings on masculinity and its failings: men's inability to communicate, their inability to form good relationships, their tendency to desert their offspring, their affinity with crime and with anti-social behaviour. By contrast, endless pages were devoted to subjects like women's greater communication skills and more caring attitudes. The impression created was that if men are the problem, then women are probably the answer.

These views are present even in the most powerful echelons of society. Harriet Harman was social security minister in the first year of Tony Blair's government. Indeed, until being moved aside she was often held up as evidence of women finally reaching senior and powerful positions within a government.

While an MP in opposition she wrote a book, *The Century Gap* (1993), in which she describes the gap between civilized and competent women who are ready for the next century and the underdeveloped men who are not. This is so much a part of accepted rhetoric that it came as no surprise, when all the statistics about male depression, male unemployment and boys' underachievement emerged, to hear one well-known feminist, Anna Coote (director of the Institute of Public Policy Research), sum up the state of modern feminism in the following terms: 'I love the fact that young women are more relaxed and take for granted that they are better than boys' (*Guardian*, 13 May 1997). Helen Wilkinson from Demos, ever ready with the handy statistic, claims: '40% of women believe that women are naturally superior to men.'

New Age philosophies must bear some responsibility for popularizing these views. They provided an incredibly simplistic version of history and culture which chimed in with a number of anxieties in the 1980s, especially about health, nature and unchecked technological development. In this simplistic account, women are associated with all that is natural, caring and holistic while men are associated with everything man-made, technological and destructive. Women's greater sensitivity, kindliness and concern for others is because the process of childbirth is meant to put women more closely in touch with nature. It is a view that equates the feminine with the positive and the masculine with the negative, and many of its exponents hope for a New Age when feminine values will triumph.

New Age philosophy has a natural affinity with left-wing and feminist ideas, but these views crop up across a whole spectrum of thinkers whose affiliations with feminism are far from obvious. The consensus is that males are uncouth, uncivilized and barbaric. Janet Daley, a right-wing columnist, regularly denounces the unappealing aspects of masculinity with the implicit assumption of the superiority of women. 'Young boys', she wrote in *The Times* in the wake of the Bulger killing, 'will degenerate quite naturally into barbarism without adult supervision,' adding, 'Had half (or even some) of the lost children in William Golding's novel been female, the terrible denoue-ment of *Lord of the Flies* would not have been credible.'

Since she wrote this, the furore surrounding Mary Bell's memoirs may have reminded her that while gender will affect how anger, aggression and sadism are expressed, violent acts by children are not the monopoly of any one gender, any more than they are in adults. Nevertheless, there will be an uphill struggle to reverse the tide of clichés on the relative merits of the sexes. They have become so much part of the media wall-paper that we no longer even notice when assumptions about women's superiority are used to justify extreme contempt and hostility towards men. By 1996, when Channel 4 launched *The Girlie Show*, its entire premise was that women are sassy and men are incompetent nerds. The show's trailers announced a show where 'girls are girls and boys are nervous'. And just to show how much more sensitive and egalitarian women are when on top, *The Girlie Show* ran items on 'wanker of the week', and 'viewers' husbands', a women's version of the regular feature in porn magazines. The pictures were either cat-called or held up as in some way disgusting.

Judy Rumbold gave a particularly clear instance of this when she turned to the subject of relationships between young women and older men. She wrote: 'I am 32 and the prospect of sleeping with anyone ten years older than me, *max*, makes my stomach turn. Call me narrow minded but my reservations are purely physical. Weird things happen to genitals. Awful ravages occur in the jowl department. Smells develop, tea smells, tweedy tobacco smells, dental smells' (*Guardian*, 1993). If any man wrote about an older woman in these offensive terms, women would be quite rightly outraged. This article doesn't just point out how unfair it is that older men can attract younger women, it is doing to men a whole series of things that women did not like having done to them. It makes them seem disgusting just for growing old and it's an uncomfortable read because it cruelly conjures up images of vulnerability.

This goes beyond a challenge to male authority. What was overvalued is now undervalued; indeed, it is the subject of contempt and disgust. It implies that masculinity is a problem, sometimes even in and of itself disgusting, its essential repulsiveness becoming more and more evident as men age. Somehow women, through their moral superiority, have acquired the right to say things which would be branded sexist if spoken by men. This is a '90s version of *Animal Farm*: two legs good, three legs bad.

Essential female goodness, by contrast, is generally agreed to manifest itself early. It is widely (and wrongly) assumed that little girls are much 'easier' than little boys, which showed up clearly when the issue of sex selection in pregnancy first erupted in 1992. Among the many recent technological innovations around fertility, selecting the sex of one's offspring at first seemed one of the least controversial. Set beside using the ova of aborted foetuses to aid artificial conception, choosing whether your baby is a boy or a girl seems pretty harmless. Indeed, in 1992 the Ethics Committee of the British Medical Association at first approved the technique, recommending that the BMA should grant a licence to a clinic which claimed to guarantee your preferred choice; they thought it was a 'a morally acceptable form of family planning'.

To the surprise of the Ethics Committee, their recommendations were thrown out by doctors who feared that sex selection would become a eugenical Pandora's box. Doctors feared it would open up the way for engineering other characteristics on the basis of social or personal preference. But they also recognized a widespread popular fear that sex selection would 'distort the demography'. The doctors assumed that, given the choice, the whole of British society would be quickly turned into the Garrick Club with a massive preference for boys. One Tory MPs even tried to get a Bill through Parliament outlawing sex selection. He claimed it would inevitably 'discriminate against women' – not something that usually bothers people of his political persuasions.

In fact, these fears proved to be wildly inaccurate. Evidence on sex preferences in the wider population points in the opposite direction. In a survey conducted in 1992, the Centre for Family Research in Cambridge found a decided preference for girls. This came as no surprise to me. For one thing, I had recently researched an article about children in care for whom adoption agencies found it almost impossible to find homes. Nine times out of ten, these were boys, generally perceived as having much more difficult and frightening ways of expressing the difficulties they had met in their lives.

I had also encountered this in more directly personal ways. When pregnant with my first child I lost count of the number of people who assumed I would prefer a girl and wished me good luck. Shortly after the baby, a boy, was born, I was cornered by a well-known feminist who quite seriously told me how, in her observation of her own daughter, everything feminism had ever said was true. All the boy children she knew were brutish, aggressive and difficult. Her own daughter and all the other girls were accommodating and kind.

More recently, a whole spate of articles and books on the subject of fathering have confirmed the same prejudice, at least among the chattering classes. In one recent newspaper article, several male writers were asked about their feelings about their daughters. All repeated this stereotype, including Martin Amis, who rhapsodized on the specialness of having a baby daughter. He described himself as feeling freer in expressing his tenderness with her, and the fact that her play is gentler and more sensitive. Women have over the past two decades become the favoured sex, sentimentalized as morally superior, emotionally more capable and generally much nicer than men. 'The feminine, and everything loosely associated with it, is in the ascendant,' said Juliette Mead in the *Daily Mail* (17 September 1977). However much women bewail their disadvantages, most end up saying how glad they are to be female, how much they want daughters rather than difficult sons. A Gallup survey conducted for the *Daily Telegraph* (3 February 1994) to ascertain how women feel about 'their role and status' in the 1990s summed it up: 'Nine out of ten women are happy to have been born female.'

There are some extremely negative effects, not just in the

disparagement of men, but in this glorification of women. At the forefront is the way it fixes masculinity and femininity as involving certain limiting and misleading characteristics. In ascribing all violence, aggression, lack of sensitivity, ruthlessness and so on to men and all the constructive, sensitive, kindly attributes to women, there's been a reinforcing of extraordinarily old-fashioned views about the sexes. Maybe now there's a higher value put on feminine characteristics such as communicativeness and consideration, but these are the very same qualities which the Victorians claimed were 'natural' and used to justify women's confined and subordinate status.

This is absurd on so many levels. It rehashes clichés of the moral superiority of women and overlooks both what is negative in stereotypical female behaviour *and* the fact that some feminine behaviour can be as bad as men's. Not to mention the nonsense of categorizing men's behaviour and contribution to history in that way. Nature is a case in point. Current environmental politics seem to be advanced far more by groups like Friends of the Earth, which is prepared to engage in scientific and political debate, than by any amount of mystical gobbledegook about women and nature.

Again it was the debate about sex selection which showed just how stereotypical the views of the sexes are. In a television programme shown at the time of the debate on licensing sex-selection clinics, a number of parents were interviewed about their reasons for wanting to influence the sex of their child (*The London Programme*, Carlton 1993). One mother described herself as 'desperate for a little girl'. Already the mother of five boys, she was willing to pay £1,500 (the average cost of treatment), even though her husband was unemployed at the time. Among her reasons for wanting a girl were, 'Boys go their own way, but girls stick closer to home . . . You can go window shopping with them', and 'You can dress them up in fancy clothes and ribbons, and just love them so much'.

Shopping also featured in the fantasies of another woman seeking treatment. She wanted a daughter because she had such a good relationship with her mother: 'She's my best friend.

We go on shopping trips together.' She added that her four-year-old boy didn't want to be dragged around the shops looking at earrings. Both women seemed to be looking for a child who would be like themselves. They both wanted a companion for life, to share interests in 'feminine' pursuits and enter a feminine community. It's not exactly footbinding awaiting these girls, but it is a sort of Barbie Doll hell. The preconceptions about feminine characteristics here are incredibly limited. Desperation for a child of a particular sex is often desperation for particular characteristics which, through prejudice, you refuse to allow the other sex.

Womanism has taken hold. There is widespread agreement: girls are less difficult, less repugnant, less dangerous, much nicer – the morally superior sex. Womanism celebrates women's positive qualities and rejects the possibility of women collaborating in unpleasantness. Womanism eschews difficult questions, like how far women themselves are capable of participating in and even initiating horrendous crimes. When Rosemary West came to trial for the multiple murders which she and her husband Fred West had committed over a period of twenty years, the public were confronted with a vision of a woman fully involved in some of the most brutal crimes of the century. Yet there was still endless questioning about how far she might have been forced to participate in crimes against her will. Had she been bullied by a man who was then too cowardly to face the consequences? Had she perhaps not even known what was going on? It was astonishing how difficult it was for people to accept her full and knowing involvement. Yet because the belief in women's subordinate position is so widely accepted, it is equally believed that a woman would never be an equal partner or initiator of transgressive or anti-social behaviour.

This tendency to justify anything women do by reference to a previous history of oppression is particularly problematic when it translates into the arena of women's 'rights'. There have been some amazingly lavish excuses made for women's behaviour when it is thought to make a contribution to changing perceptions of and opportunities for women. The rhetoric of 'girl power' is a good instance. The Spice Girls coined the phrase as a bit of promotional fun but it passed quickly into the wider culture as a good label to use in any situation in which girls might be putting themselves forward in new, brash and 'unfeminine' ways. 'Challenging the stereotypes', though, can cover a multitude of sins. Some challenges might be useful for easing the constraints which some girls and women still experience, but others might be ways of adding moral justification to behaviour which is just self-seeking.

Although we are meant to be a society committed to equality and to tempering shows of power by one group over another, we have been remarkably reluctant to criticize the idea that the assertion of women's power somehow advances the cause for all women. We disregard 'girls on top' rhetoric as a necessary corrective for all the centuries of oppression. Women's bid to be more powerful than men is playful, a façade, because women's power could never be abusive and harmful. Asserting power becomes in and of itself acceptable just because women once lacked the kind of power men had. Indeed, it is the previous lack of power, their victim status, which gives some of the protagonists their conviction of moral righteousness. With some issues this produces double standards, most blatantly around sex. If boys asserted the same desire to have sexual power over women, we'd want them shut away as potential rapists.

There are plenty of areas in contemporary society where this mishmash of women's righteousness and women's rights is being mobilized for ends which have nothing to do with the aims of an egalitarian society. In 1997 Nicola Horlick published a book called *Can You Have It All?* The book's title was a self-conscious reference to the question which had long haunted feminism: can women combine motherhood and work and, by implication, are they right to? Horlick was an unlikely character to join a feminist debate. A high-earning city financier, she had only come to attention when, sacked from one bank for apparently poaching her team of staff, the media suddenly discovered a mother of five, earning over a million a year. Horlick's answer to the question in her title was an unequivocal yes; with help from an old-fashioned nanny, whose duties would have made a Victorian servant look idle, rich women have the right to try and have it all.

The discourse of women's rights can be equally problematic coming from the opposite end of the social spectrum. In September 1995, the BBC found an interviewee called 'Sarah' to illustrate the government's concern with benefits to single mothers and the problems the CSA (Child Support Agency) was having in getting fathers to pay maintenance. 'Sarah' instantly became the focus of right-wing tabloid hatred. 'There are thousands of women like me,' she warned in the *Daily Mirror*. Sarah was the mother of six children by four different fathers, currently living off benefit and trying to get a sterilization reversed so that she could now have a child with her new husband, a convicted sex offender. Her welfare bill was £100,0000 a year and her defence of her position simple: 'No one will tell me how many kids I can have.'

In the furore that followed, there was no shortage of feminist commentators pointing out that Sarah was hardly typical; most single mothers have been abandoned and many are often desperate to escape from the benefit culture. Such a woman was simply being mobilized to scare people into imagining the worst and no one would challenge the rights of men or rich women in such situations. All of which is true. While pointing this out, though, no one actually said that her notion of rights was a travesty of feminism, and at one level it wasn't. No one was prepared to criticize Sarah because there's a squeamishness about women's 'rights' – anything a woman does to overthrow the old restrictions must be right – so no one will even ask whether children are disadvantaged by such a situation.

What started as a need to support women's rights has become the need to support women because they are right. Women's rights were the central platform of both Sarah's and Nicola Horlick's claims, but there was little here of feminism's more egalitarian, democratic concerns. Instead, this is a highjacking of the discourse of women's rights to an individual's own ends: Horlick to justify her actions at work as the actions of a strong woman in pursuit of her objectives, and Sarah to justify the emotional disorder of her life. Both also grabbed at a discourse of victimhood. Horlick, when extensively ridiculed by the press, cast herself as the victim of prejudice against women and mothers in a male chauvinist world. 'Sexism has a lot to do with it,' she complained. 'They will not let go until they destroy me!' (*Observer*, 12 October 1997). Sarah cast herself as the victim of the state which denied her the right to have another child by refusing to pay for a sterilization reversal. For both, motherhood was an issue of rights; women have a right to children, and those rights appear more important than the needs and the rights of the children they had created.

To confuse rights with a state of moral righteousness based on women's previous position as the oppressed, avoids the more difficult questions of how you define what is right in more ambiguous times. As we shall see in the following chapters, whenever womanism crops up as an answer to questions about how the sexes should behave, it obliterates the more complex questions.

Claiming the moral righteousness of the oppressed to assert dubious rights is a refusal to face up to the possibility both of men's vulnerability and of women's potency. It refuses to accept women's role in constructing objectionable aspects of masculinity and it justifies everything done in the name of woman, often at the same time denying men the right to do or express themselves in the same way. Feminism is often used to give womanism credence, although they are not the same thing. Womanism takes root when the complexities of feminism are allowed to wither. It's a simplistic reduction of reality, providing easy answers to difficult questions, such as blaming 'masculinity' for social problems, or defending the indefensible just because questions of women's rights are brought into the picture. As I show in subsequent chapters, it produces misinterpretations of society and is mobilized to attack the most vulnerable men. But before exploring this further, we need to look at how men have reacted to this triumphalism.

THE 'MASCULINIST' REACTION

Never let it be said that women have been alone in champoning the authority of one sex over the other. There have been plenty of men doing this, alongside their female sympathizers who have matched them every step of the way. Faced with the contrast between their own gender uncertainties and the triumphalist rhetoric of some women, the conclusion has been drawn that the pendulum has swung too far: we must be living in a matriarchy. For these, the preoccupation has been with reasserting the lost powers of men. Indeed, the 1990s saw not only the emergence of a Men's Movement no longer sympathetic to feminism, but also a number of political and social theorists for whom restoring male authority had become the critical element in curing society's ills.

The Men's Movement in the 1970s had always been a sympathetic counterpart to feminism, ready to take any criticism which women felt inclined to throw at it. After all, there were centuries of oppression to reverse. Some of the earlier feminist conferences in Britain had crèches run by men, usually supportive partners of women involved in the conferences. Raphael Samuels, the Marxist historian, was often seen feeding babies and cutting out paper shapes. Looking back, I imagine many feminists feel uncomfortable about how readily men's efforts at helping out were disparaged. At the time, these men were made the butt of jokes about currying sexual favours or suspected for their willingness to reverse the roles.

The journals which emerged from groups at this time were also easy targets for women. *Achilles Heel* in the early days was a forum largely for discussing the restraints of the sort of upbringing which had left men so 'incapable'. A kind of abject and self-effacing willingness to make it up to women was what haunted these early publications. It seemed to draw from women an awful kind of castrating vengefulness. Women chided these men; why didn't they just get on with giving support and stop talking about it? Time has made these men look very virtuous.

Men's consciousness-raising groups continued to meet through the 1980s and in America they boomed, boosted by the flourishing growth movement with its interest in humanistic psychotherapy and the idea of working on yourself to become a more 'fulfilled' human being. But by the late 1980s the Men's Movement had begun to give voice to some of the discontents arising from a changing economy. What emerged in the '90s was a movement that was increasingly masculinist, less interested in supporting women's changes than in re-establishing masculine identity and, in some cases, even male supremacy.

It was from the culture of personal growth seminars that Robert Bly's *Iron John* emerged. Neil Spencer described *Iron John* as 'the opening salvo of a debate about male identity – concerning fatherhood, the raising of sons and the male response to feminism – which has become progressively louder and more bad-tempered' (*Observer*, 17 December 1995). Although *Iron John* has many sympathetic references to feminism, ultimately it is concerned with reasserting a traditional male identity. The earlier Men's Movement had opened up the possibility of looking at masculinity in the way women looked at femininity – as a construct, a role, ultimately a performance. Now Bly asserted the need to rediscover a lost masculinity which would be vital in standing up to the new dominance of women.

Bly had spent many years on the circuit of these alternative self-growth seminars before becoming well-known as the 'leader of the men's movement'. This happened when he stopped running growth classes for both sexes based on fairy tales and started running men-only groups. His presentation of 'Iron John' as an ancient myth of a now threatened masculinity was an instant success, so Bly wrote up his ideas as a book.

Women had much sport with Robert Bly when *Iron John* was first published in Britain, especially with accounts of his workshops. Suggestions that men should meet in the woods, sometimes naked, to try and get in touch with 'the hairy man within' caused much hilarity. It seemed an awful lot of trouble to go to to find out something which most men seemed never to have lost. Accounts emerged from workshops of Bly and his followers encouraging men to wear bandages on the parts of their bodies they can remember hurting to explore 'the male wound'. To women still engaged in more pragmatic egalitarian political projects, these scenes of mass male vulnerability seemed uncomfortably like a call for the return of Florence Nightingale.

Iron John, however, is a more complex and interesting book than this suggests. Superficially it is powerful and libertarian. The use of the central myth of Iron John, linked to other myths, legends and religions, is surprisingly evocative of a boy's journey to adulthood. Bly seems to have a strong intuitive grasp of how boys develop and spots the way this expresses itself in a number of myths. Yet the framework of *Iron John* is disagreeable. Bly is convinced that contemporary men have become soft, lost touch with their masculinity, because they have allowed themselves to become passive in relation to increasingly powerful women:

> in the seventies I began to see all over the country a phenomenon that we might call the 'soft male' ... They are lovely, valuable people – I like them – they're not interested in harming the earth or starting wars ... But many of these men are not happy. You quickly note the lack of energy in them. Ironically you often see these men with strong women who positively radiate energy ... he himself has little vitality to offer.

Bly's project is to restore the vitality which he calls masculinity; men should be put back in touch with their instinctive quickness, resolve and strength which have been sapped by women-dominated cultures. Bly insists that he is not anti-women but his book voices a fear of the suffocating, cloying mother

127

and this ultimately extends to all women. He describes the pull of the feminine and the maternal in terms of the 'swamp', something which pulls men down, confuses them and ultimately drowns them. Societies where women have too much power trap men irrevocably. He sees initiation rites and myths of male journeys and quests as expressions of an ancient truth of the male journey *away* from the mother towards a masculine identity.

Bly is the most coherent, best-known and probably the most liberal of the men who began to respond to what was seen as an assault on masculinity. Others had less sympathy for why feminism had happened in the first place. The 1990s bore witness to increasing numbers of men's groups which were no longer interested in redefining masculinity alongside the changes which women were making, but with opposing the emasculation of men by the new matriarchy. Increasingly the talk was of discrimination. Michael Newland, founder of the US group, the White Brothers, complained that 'no other group . . . identifiable by gender and race has suffered as much discrimination as white men' (quoted in the *Guardian*, 4 August 1993). Under the title 'No-one loves me any more, cries the great White male', the right-wing tabloid *Daily Mail* reported: 'A survey for Newsweek magazine reveals 52% of white males believe they are losing their influence in the fields of entertainment, the arts and style' (23 March 1993). Suzanne Moore, a British journalist writing in the *Guardian*, wittily dubbed it 'victim envy'.

Certainly the reactionary, anti-women element is all too clear in other manifestations of Men's Movement nostalgia for male supremacy. Promise Keepers is one such recent men's group which is explicit about the disastrous emasculation caused by the pursuit of equal relationships between the sexes. Promise Keepers consists of American Christians. In 1995 it boasted 280,000 members; by 1997, 700,000 attended a rally in Washington. One of its explicit aims is to restore 'male leadership' and members pledge themselves to physical and spiritual purity, talking of struggles and resistance. Their founder, Bill

McCarthy, formed the movement following a dream of men promising to eschew adultery, to take responsibility and to lead their families out of America's social wilderness. They use sports stadia and sportsmen as cheerleaders to create what they call an environment of 'godly masculinity'.

The theme of male grievances is not unfamiliar in Britain through the works of David Thomas and Neil Lyndon. Their woes, however, were so obviously self-regarding that they did not merit much serious attention. In his book *No More Sex War: The Failures of Feminism* (1992), Neil Lyndon seemed to blame all the discomfort he felt in his own life – the disintegration of his marriage and the loss of custody of his child – on the emasculation of men by the monstrous regiment of women, 'the sisterhood' as he spitefully calls it. In *Not Guilty: In Defence of Modern Man* (1993), David Thomas also rued the emasculation of men, blind apparently to the extraordinary advantages and privileges which his own background had given him.

Lyndon and Thomas both did themselves a disservice by writing such unpleasant books. Both sounded aggrieved, isolated and bitter; both adopted the discourse of the victim. Lyndon's case is inflamed by his grievances against changes in family law which appear to weight divorce and custody settlements in women's favour, grievances strongly influenced by his own divorce and loss of custody which were extensively aired in the British press.

These two books are very specific, growing out of bitter personal histories in a particular milieu, but there's also something symptomatic about them. Both link the more nebulous loss of male cultural authority with actual changes in the law which have undermined some patriarchal rights. They are convinced that the combination of gender uncertainty which feminism has placed on them and the shifts in family policy which now appear to favour women, amount to a victimization of men. The UK's tiny Men's Movement would agree. Dr Roger Whitcomb, its chair, says: 'The pendulum has swung too far in favour of women – it's time for men to demand their rights' (*New Statesman*, 14 August 1995). As in Lyndon's book, the focus is on the loss of men's rights within the family, and like him they go on to generalize from this into other areas where they now see men as disadvantaged, citing issues such as date rape, sexual harassment, images in the media and so on.

There's another way in which Lyndon's and Thomas's books are symptomatic. Like other books about masculinity which emerged in the 1990s, their writing is overshadowed by an unconscious preoccupation with an image of lost *power*, especially paternal power. Regret or even hostility for an all-powerful mother is counterposed by a deep nostalgia for a time when the father was less vulnerable, more potent. When David Thomas and Neil Lyndon start talking about fathers – their loss of authority and their displacement by the monstrous army of feminist matriarchs – the referent is all too clear: their own fathers. Lyndon's dialogue with his own father, old and emasculated by his son's sexual adventures, erupts suddenly but seems explicable in terms of Lyndon's desire to gain, by this book, moral authority in the eyes of his own son. The book is dedicated to this son 'in the hope that he will one day understand'.

Meanwhile, Thomas publicly attributes his disagreement with feminism to the fact that, in feminists' eyes, his father represented the ultimate patriarchal authority. Yet David Thomas saw his father as an increasingly vulnerable old man; why couldn't feminists see that men can be vulnerable? Thomas's father was a diplomat; even more surprising than feminism's apparent blind-spot is Thomas's inability to separate institutional power from an increasingly frail old man. More to the point, it is tempting to see Thomas's conviction that women now have more power than men as a misplaced lament for the lost patriarchal power of his own vulnerable father.

This preoccupation with the lost authority of the father, this nostalgia for paternal authority, has become an ever-more insistent and explicit theme in the 1990s. Robert Bly's *Sibling Society*, written in 1996, linked his theories about the threat to masculine identity with the widespread concern about anti-social males; the explanation for both was the marginalization or even overthrow of the father, the loss of parental authority, and the consequent lack of masculine identification. *Sibling Society* contends that America is becoming a society of orphans.

In all these accounts there is a total reversal of the feminist project. Men have become conscious of themselves as men and of the criticisms of masculinity, but this is now seen as a negative thing. They assume that this loss is the reason for a number of other losses across the rest of society – in employment, in the family, in general opportunities – when what has been happening in these areas has many different causes. For this group, though, the discomfort men are feeling is due to the challenge to their moral authority having been implemented as a systematic programme of discrimination; so they adopt all those attributes which women claimed for themselves – they say they are powerless, victims of injustice, and economically disadvantaged. Women's triumphalism is, in their eyes, the sign of the new matriarchy. The response to all this is the reassertion of old certainties of male and female behaviour and roles – male authority in the family and across society. Masculinist ideas reassert the primacy of gender and insist that the outcome of the struggle between the sexes will be all-important in determining the well-being of society.

Commentators tend to dismiss the Men's Movement as cranky and marginal, but it is a mirror-image of womanism and both have penetrated current thinking on social crisis. Many of the most influential commentators, policy-makers and social theorists tussling with contemporary problems dip into the storehouse of these gender debates. But 'men strong, women gentle' is really no more help in understanding where we are than 'women good, men bad'. We live in a world where the oppressors can be vulnerable and the victims can have power. It is more equal and more confusing. Reducing these complexities to simple polarities can be incredibly damaging. Nowhere is this more evident than in the three social issues currently causing most concern: young men and boys, parenting, and sexual behaviour. In the following chapters I look at how womanism and its reaction get in the way of understanding what has really been going on.

It would be easy to laugh off womanism, with its handy cor-
ralling of negative human attributes into the male of the
species, were it not for the ugly way in which masculinity has
recently become the focus for some of society's darkest fears
and imaginings about social disintegration and disorder.
Nowhere has the anti-male rhetoric had more unfortunate
effects that among the most vulnerable groups of men – the
young, the unemployed and the poor. And nowhere has
the feminist rhetoric about men's power seemed more
hollow. In the 1990s, it was not only the single mother who
attracted a negative press; the opprobrium she received was
nothing compared to that heaped on the head of the unruly
male. The 'yob' or 'lout' was both symbol and cause of our
moral decline. Feminism was not responsible for putting
him there, but it certainly played a part in validating the class
fears which fuelled the demonizing of impoverished young
men.

'Yob' was once a slang insult, but now it is used by tabloids
and quality papers alike as a descriptive category. Incorporating
other breeds such as lager louts, football hooligans and joyrid-
ers, the yob is a species of young, white, working-class males
who, if the British media are to be believed, are more common
(and younger) than ever before. The yob is foul-mouthed, irresponsible, probably unemployed and violent. The yob hangs
around council estates where he terrorizes the local inhabitants,
possibly in the company of his pit-bull terrier. He 'fathers'
children rather than cares for them. He is often drunk, probably uses drugs and is likely to be involved in crime, including

domestic violence. He is the ultimate expression of macho values; mad, bad and dangerous.

The yob is the bogeyman of the 1990s, hated and feared with a startling intensity by the British middle class. Jeremy Kingston, in *The Times*, reckons such men are 'crapulous louts'. Paul Theroux, commenting on a day out at the seaside, said 'It was the size of their heads I found alarming ... A head without any hair is a small thing.' Simon Heffer of the *Daily Telegraph* echoed Peter Lilley's outrageous comments that not even women of their own social class can tolerate such ghastly specimens: 'Nobody wants to marry a yob because he is boorish, lazy and unemployable.' Jack Straw promises to wipe such undesirables off our streets.

As fears about moral decline and social disorder grew in the early 1990s, the language in which such young men are described – louts, scum, beasts – could be heard across the political spectrum. It appeared in an extreme form in *Sun* editorials and in a modified version in sombre discussions of youth crime. More surprisingly, it appeared in some feminist writings on contemporary masculinity. Individual men disappear in this language into a faceless mob.

There is nothing new about young men being the focus of social fears and anxieties, but in the last decade this hostility towards young working-class or unemployed men has escalated. Until the visible human tragedies of the Hillsborough disaster challenged perceptions of the football crowd, it had been the football hooligan who embodied anti-social disorder. Afterwards, as the policy towards football fans changed, concern shifted to other slightly different areas of male behaviour. Janet Daley, writing in *The Times* (16 June 1992), claimed in shockingly bigoted terms that 'the drunken neanderthals' who had previously used 'soccer as a pretext for a more entertaining blood sport' had now discovered joyriding, 'disinherited by an education system that sees no need to introduce them to higher literacy (or even to speak their own language properly) proletarian children have found another route to glory'.

In the late 1980s, with dramatically increasing crime statistics, the panic expanded to include 'drunkenness' and 'rural hooliganism'. The generic term was 'lager louts' and their activities abroad were a favourite theme: typically the *Daily Express* cried, 'shame of Costa louts', continuing, 'Here we go, here we go, here we go ... it's summer in Sunny Spain and the drinking is easy for El Hooligan' (8 August 1989). Scenes of violence at foreign football matches called forth acres of tabloid anguish. 'The animals shame us all', claimed the *Daily Mail* (7 September 1989). 'Every decent Englishman will hang his head in shame this morning after loathsome animals masquerading as football fans again dragged the name of our country into the gutter' (*Sun*, 7 September 1989).

This contemptuous hostility could be seen again in the scorn heaped on the heads of pit-bull owners at the height of the dangerous dogs scare of 1991. Even quality papers carried sneering interviews with men who called their dogs Kosh or Tyson and 'who are usually between 18 and 25, with short hair and tattoos, dressed in shell suits with trainers'. This insistent view of the yob as morally delinquent – idle, criminal, unemployable, and (a very '90s inflection) unmarriageable – would cause outcry if such language was used to refer to a race or to women. But when in the mid-1990s one judge referred to an 'epidemic of shiftless young men' as 'a menace which has got to stop', no one disagreed with him.

The yob is not, in fact, a new phenomenon. For centuries, poor men and crime have been connected in the public imagination, particularly in times of economic hardship. Late nineteenth-century Britain saw the rise of the 'residuum', an underclass of the poor whose lifestyle and morals were seen as dangerously anti-social. A half-century later, it was the turn of the teddy boys, and mods and rockers who brought the atmosphere of criminal gangland warfare into a society which believed itself to be united. Motorbikes, black leather and booze signalled young men on the rampage, spitting in the face of 1950s' respectability. Contemporary fears, however, have a new element. There's a growing belief that there is something in masculinity itself which inclines poor young men to anti-social behaviour. 'No matter which way you cut the statistics,' wrote feminist Angela Phillips, 'the factor that is always closely correlated with criminality is the presence of a Y-chromosome' (*Guardian*, 23 November 1993).

This is a recent twist to an old story. Contemporary theories of a social underclass draw on this long history of male outcast groups. The 1990s' image of the council estate, with its gangs of alienated youths, abandoned mothers and violent homes, drug-dealing, drinking and chronic crime, is an update of an earlier vision of the dark side of Britain's social landscape. Today's commentators speak in truly Dickensian terms.

> I have been travelling through that other Britain which the comfortable and contented among us neither know nor want to know. It is the Britain of 'sink' housing estates; a world of ugly, harsh buildings of tower blocks with urine-soaked lifts, of vast open spaces strewn with litter, of 30-yard benefit queues. It is a world of desperate, often workless young men, whose natural aggression and desire to prove themselves has soured into volcanic anger; of deserted single mothers and fugitive fathers. (*Daily Mail*, 27 July 1992)

Images of the underclass as a cancer likely to destroy the benign social order abound, as do representations of the yobbish element as primitive beasts attacking the social fold. A recent advertising campaign, warning car-owners to lock their cars, showed snarling hyenas circling a vehicle on a dark night. The message is clear; the dangerous dogs of the British poor are everywhere. These images would not have entered mainstream intellectual and political life if not legitimated, and in Britain two discourses in particular have provided them with a respectable gloss. One is the underclass theory, the other – more surprisingly – the quasi-feminist critique of masculinity.

The views on the underclass of the US sociologist Charles Murray had considerable influence on the Conservative government of John Major between 1992 and 1997. The government was drawn to his ideas because they reinforced a traditional view that crime and poverty resulted from moral rather than economic failures. Such ideas still lurk in the more liberal views of Tony Blair and Jack Straw. They use more humane, less accusatory terms, such as 'social exclusion', but rather than see this exclusion as the effect of class inequalities (in terms of access to jobs, education, decent housing), they also include a moral element. They talk of a deprived and excluded group, but also a group of dispossessed people, no longer sharing dominant (middle-class) social values and morality, who must be reintegrated into society.

Murray, whose ideas were formulated in America, turned his attention to Britain on the invitation of the *Sunday Times* (24 May 1994). He argues that Britain, like America, is suffering from severe social fracturing with a resultant escalation of violence and crime. The underclass – a rump group unable to escape from poverty – are responsible for that increase in crime and threaten the very basis of social cohesion.

Crucial in the formation of the underclass, according to Murray, is the rise of the single mother. In the lower-income groups, especially those dependent on welfare, marriage has declined and illegitimate births have increased. Children born in such situations are deprived of economic and emotional stability and parental authority, making them more liable to become criminals. They perpetuate the cycle, too. Daughters of these families, Murray says, are more likely themselves to have illegitimate children, thereby increasing the numbers who will live by crime and violence.

Much attention has been paid to the way Murray appears to blame single mothers for the rise of the underclass – something with which even the right-wing and tactless Virginia Bottomley took issue – but his real social threat is male. 'Young males', he wrote in the *Sunday Times*, 'are essentially barbarians who are civilised by marriage.' In American underclass theory, this had a particularly racist formulation – blame was placed on the young single black woman, but the fear was of the black male. In Britain the fear was more of an indeterminate masculine horde. Underclass theory sees men as the perpetrators of violent crime, they are disordered and anti-social, sated in the trashy images of a video culture. Murray dubs them the 'New Rabble', primitive beasts civilized only by women and marriage. His views are happily endorsed by middle-class opinion formers: 'The underclass', wrote Andrew Neil in 1995,

> is not a degree of poverty ... It is a type of poverty; it covers those who no longer share the norms and aspirations of society. It is a ticking time bomb we do not know how to diffuse. It is at the root of our yob culture, the coarsening of our society, and most of the upsurge in criminality. (*Sunday Times*, 28 May 1995)

These ideas of an underclass are seriously inadequate as a way of understanding either why crime is escalating or what is happening to social class and feelings of community. Social theorist Professor Jeffrey Weeks refutes Murray's ideas of the underclass as 'both pejorative and stigmatising. It reduces very complex changes to a single cause – the breakdown of marriage – and inevitably leads to scapegoating' (interview with author). In other words, this is a very reductive version of what is happening in society, one which scapegoats rather than recognizes or understands shared human desires and aspirations. What's more, Murray's evidence is very shaky. As Professor Ruth Lister says: 'Most illegitimate births are registered by both parents, and usually this implies as much commitment as a marriage. It also assumes that single parenting can never be adequate, and that the consequences will be crime and disruptive behaviour – neither of which is backed up by evidence. The concept is extraordinarily imprecise' (interview with author).

Imprecision, however, never stopped an idea taking hold. And the myth of yobbism exerts its grip far beyond the circle of Murray's articulate supporters. Hatred of yobs has become entangled in a wider hostility towards men; a hostility fuelled by a feminist critique of masculinity. It is the maleness of the yobs, and particularly the hyped-up machismo that they represent, which is often seen as the main problem. 'Crime is largely a male monopoly,' writes Andrew Neil, 'and within that young men are the dominant force ... They are the children of the underclass and they are in the process of spawning their own in far greater numbers.' Drawing on pop psychology or biology, journalists now often blame joyriding and football hooliganism on 'testosterone levels', and macho cults. Decrying the machismo of impoverished men has become a favourite media pastime.

As I have argued in previous chapters, some of the less pleasant aspects of masculinity deserve to be mocked, but when this disparagement of all things male is linked to the poor – to those who are most disadvantaged in the current economy – the result is much more problematic. Beatrix Campbell's *Goliath: Britain's Dangerous Places* (1993) is a feminist text which reveals many of the worrying consequences of pinning crime and unrest on working-class men. *Goliath* was written in the wake of the 1991 riots across Britain, and the general thesis is that 'the great unspoken in the crime angst of the eighties and nineties is that it is a phenomenon of masculinity'. Campbell sees economic deprivation as creating two types of people: 'active citizens' (women) and the dispossessed (men). Teenage girls have the option of becoming parents, and, according to Campbell, this automatically inclines them towards solidarity. But young men turn against their community, burning down community centres and shops, burgling the houses on the estates, and terrorizing women.

Campbell thinks unemployment consigns men to the world of women. It denies them institutions and activities where men have previously congregated and escaped. Now they are banished to the same marginal family existence in which women have always lived. But men refuse to share that space. They turn against it in a wave of macho aggression. Campbell sees unemployment as unleashing and endorsing extreme forms of masculinity: 'Unemployment reveals a mode of masculinity, whereas the commonsense notion has been that it causes a crisis of masculinity.' In particular, it is the trashy excesses of mass culture which fan their brutality: 'surrounded by a macho propaganda more potent in its penetration of young men's hearts and minds than at any time in history – they were soaked in globally transmitted images and ideologies of butch and brutal solutions to life's difficulties' (ibid.). In other words, unemployment does not fracture masculinity but rolls back the stops to an unfettered expression of that masculinity.

It is this celebration of masculinity which, in Campbell's view, explains the attraction of crime. Criminality is 'one of the cultures in which young men acquire the mantle of manhood . . . young men on council estates are engaged in a militaristic culture of crime . . . They celebrate war, force and hierarchies as ways of sorting things out.' While the men turn to 'danger and destruction, women's response to the economic crisis is "survival and solidarity"'. The government does nothing to help them because, 'like battered women, the estates have been abandoned by statutory agencies and left to the mercy of their most dangerous elements'. Nor will the police cooperate with the women because the women don't count, and because the police share so many of the lads' masculine values that they mirror and thereby provoke some of the worst excesses.

There are interesting insights here, namely into the effect on men of being consigned to a domestic space without having a role in it, and especially her perception of the shared interests between young men and male hierarchies such as the police. Yet there are also some really dubious assumptions at work here. Campbell criticizes the new Right for blaming mothers for not managing their men. Yet when she says, 'the mothers were all that was between these boys and a riotous assembly. Nothing else was there to stop them,' the echoes of underclass theory are there for all to see. The 'lads', no less than Murray's underclass, appear as a dangerous mob, redeemable only by the civilizing effects of women and family.

Expectations about masculine behaviour clearly shape responses to economic deprivation. But this demonizing of men, with its implicit idealizing of women, is very simplistic. Male behaviour cannot be understood in isolation from female behaviour. It is not a question of blaming one sex or another, but of seeing how cultural patterns arise in which the 'wildness' of young men often matches the demands put on them by young women, at least before the girls 'settle down'. Many of the accounts of joyriding on the estates include girls lined up at the side watching, or being the audience to whom such exploits are later recounted. Mothers also play a complex role in the upbringing of their sons. Liverpool poet Brian Patten grew up in Toxteth, which often features in the 'underclass' theory, but doesn't recognize the picture: 'These people say that the men are very destructive, but the women could egg the men on. In my experience, if you came home having been hit, your mother told you to go out and hit back, even if you really didn't want to' (interview with author). Nick Danziger's *Danziger's Britain: A Journey to the Edge* (1997) also paints a more confused picture. The desolation he records in the cities of Britain in the 1990s is not 'caused' by the lads with the victimized women working more constructively for the communities; it has more complex causes.

When writers such as Campbell argue that 'crime and coercion are sustained by men. Solidarity and self help are sustained by women. It is as stark as that,' it isn't surprising that Conservative commentators have found support for their own hostility to 'lads'. It is more alarming to find feminist justification for this kind of hostility in New Labour's current policies on welfare, single mothers and the family. Anna Coote, for example, adviser to Harriet Harman on women's issues, wrote of 'the deep dark silence' behind the moral panic about crime, which is 'the link between men and crime' (*Cosmopolitan*, 1993). No wonder some of us are worried about what precisely lies behind New Labour's determination to get single mothers into work, to become breadwinners. Obviously to do so would reduce the benefits bill, but does it also imply giving up on men, escaping from their downward pull? There are strong echoes of Murray's ideas. Murray wants women to civilize men. New Labour's feminists want women to save themselves and leave men to it. Both regard poor men as uncivilized and women as the solution.

Feminism's critique of masculinity, which was originally intended to undermine traditional claims to male power, has now become a way of attacking the least powerful men in our society. That critiques of gender can be used in this way should warn us that they are not necessarily progressive. Women's protests against male dominance have, at other times, similarly intersected with, or even reinforced, middle-class efforts to subdue and 'civilize' the male 'underclass'. And the history of this link between feminism and efforts to 'reform' lumpen masculinity serves as a contemporary warning.

In the late nineteenth century, many philanthropic feminists raised their voices in concern about the underclass, the 'residuum', who embodied middle-class fear about urban poverty. Fear reached a peak when, in the 1880s, the Industrial Revolution badly affected many of London's traditional industries. As factory production grew in the north, London's industries found it difficult to compete. The main effect was increased casualization of labour as industrialists, faced with falling orders, tried to stabilize or maximize profits. Combined with large-scale movement from the countryside and the absence of any welfare except charity, the conditions of the urban poor were dire. Contemporary accounts describe enfeebled men lying in drunken or opium-induced stupors or gathering in terrifying groups.

Responses to this crisis varied, but overall it was agreed that the problems of the residuum were due to their own deficiencies, both physical and moral, rather than structural underemployment. A theory of urban degeneracy emerged, blaming the enfeebling dissipations of town life for creating weak and ineffectual paupers who had no work and were not fit for it. Coarse, drunken, brutish and immoral, such men were best weeded out of the social system entirely through emigration, or home labour colonies, or sterilization. This would leave a respectable or deserving poor. 'It is a shocking thing to say of men created in God's image, but it is true that the extinction of the unemployed would add to the wealth of the country,' said one leading philanthropist.

Historian Gareth Steadman Jones, who wrote the definitive study of this period, *Outcast London* (1971), says:

I was not trying to suggest that these people were lovable or that they were easy to feel solidarity with. They led short, miserable, awful lives. But then, as now, the discourse created them as a sort of 'other' whom no one respectable could identify with. That creation serves a conservatism born of fear. The main difference is that this 'other' was seen as degenerate and pathetic rather than violent. But they were still seen as a menace right across the political spectrum.'
(Interview with author)

The middle classes feared urban riots and socialist revolution. Trade union leaders dreaded the army of casual labour standing outside the gates, a constant threat to union organization. Philanthropic reformers worried about the degenerate morals of the residuum because many lived in common-law marriages and many were in overcrowded conditions which they believed encouraged incest – 'the promiscuous sty' as one of them called it.

This group of philanthropists, which included many women, particularly charity workers and housing reformers, maintained an attitude towards the poor which was often moralistic and coercive. Octavia Hill, the leading housing reformer, believed that the best way to reform 'the destructive classes' was through moral retraining offered by lady visitors. They would intrude into working-class homes and instruct the inhabitants in their duties. The exertion of this 'moral force', as Hill described it, was seen as particularly suitable for well-bred ladies with a philanthropic bent. The aim was to raise the residuum through a training in middle-class norms – sobriety, hard work, thrift and sexual continence.

Hill was not a feminist, but many other reformers were. By and large, they were equally patronizing and even more emphatic about the degeneracy of the underclass male. Feminists often forged alliances with 'respectable' working-class men in civil rights campaigns. Historian Judith Walkowitz emphasizes that 'feminists of the period were part of a general movement to construct a new model of masculinity; a model of self control, chivalry and self restraint' (interview with author).

One of the main areas in which such reforms were sought concerned domestic violence. Men of all classes beat their wives, but, as far as Victorian feminists were concerned, the problem revolved entirely around the brutishness of the proletarian male. Frances Power Cobbe, a leading campaigner against domestic violence, based her struggle on the assertion that all working-class men were violent louts. Similarly, feminists in the Sexual Purity Movement, while apparently condemning all male sexual licence and brutality towards women, were particularly punitive towards the underclass.

This hostility to the outcast poor was partly class anxiety – young, able-bodied men have always represented a threat to established interests – but then, as now, there was also a fearful animosity towards aspects of masculinity and male sexuality. Christabel Pankhurst once wrote: 'The normal woman regards the sex act as the final pledge of her faith and her love, and the idea that her husband may take a lower view of it is repulsive to her' (*The Great Scourge*, 1913). This 'lower view' was widely seen by the feminists as a primitive lust which men ought to control. Since the men of the lower classes were the lost primitives, their ability to control themselves was seen as correspondingly reduced, not helped by alcohol, overcrowding and moral fecklessness.

The 'battle against lust', as another Victorian feminist put it, thus became a battle to impose a civilized middle-class family life on what was seen as the erotic disorder of the poor. And while it is unlikely that anyone would now put it in such terms, there are startling similarities with the perception of contemporary poor men as promiscuously irresponsible, incapable of family commitments and greatly in need of moral reform in favour of 'womanly' values. Then, as now, women's response to men was conditioned by the fact that men of all classes can pose problems for women, particularly in a country whose institutions and law have been formed in a male-dominated culture. But as with the concern about yobs and louts in the

1980s and '90s, that response can often be hard to distinguish from class prejudices.

Reform efforts, directed against the underclass, including feminist efforts, persisted until the First World War when wartime mobilization transformed the feckless disreputables of the outcast poor into indispensable workers, soldiers and heroes. 'The use of the term residuum disappears during the First World War,' says Steadman Jones. 'There was a real labour shortage and men of all classes were called on to do something. Once seen doing something, they can't be seen as unemployable.' The residuum, those yobs of yesteryear, revealed itself for what it had always been: not an army of degenerate unemployables, but the under-employed who disappeared into the military and the wartime workforce. A myth died, just as the myth of yobbism would if impoverished young men of contemporary Britain were given genuine opportunities.

The yob does not, in fact, exist. Seen close up, the yob dissolves. The yob is never the boy you know – only the one you don't. As in all bigoted mythologies, the yob is that alien and bad creature against whom the familiar and the good are culturally defined; the 'them' which defines the 'us'. It is unfashionable to say this, since there seems to be widespread agreement that at the centre of social malaise today are unruly youths. Yet, as soon as any of these 'yobs' is seen close to or individually, a more complex picture emerges of individuals struggling with difficult circumstances, of pain and suffering and failed hopes just like the rest of us.

When Roddy Doyle fictionalizes the 'yob' in his novel, *Paddy Clarke, Ha Ha Ha* (1994), it isn't difficult for us to feel sympathy for Paddy, even when he pours lighter fluid into his baby brother's mouth and lights it. When he writes, 'I wanted to be hard. I wanted to wear plastic sandals and smack them on the ground and dare anyone to look at me . . . I wanted to get that far. I wanted to look at my ma and da and not feel anything. I wanted to be ready,' the links between pain and anti-social behaviour are easy to see. But even as the praise for Doyle's Booker Prize was dying down, the papers continued to hammer out stories of yobs who commit crimes because their brutish macho values are not the same as those of decent people.

To say that the yob does not exist, except as a cultural fantasy, does not mean that poor and unruly men are not a problem in British society, nor that the weak and vulnerable do not feel endangered by their behaviour. The economic guts have been ripped from large areas by the dramatic changes which the economy has undergone. In less than a generation, many men have watched an entire edifice of everyday life, built on steady work and a regular wage, crumble. In that context men suffer, as do women and families too. Children grow up feeling their parents' pain and their own helplessness. Such helplessness breeds rage and aggression. The boys' rage erupts on to the streets. Girls are likelier to remain locked in emotional violence – no less damaging for that; they turn their rage inwards – on themselves and their families. The price of this is huge, not because it creates some nameless horde but because the hopes and frustrations of whole groups of individuals have been written out of the political agenda.

It is known that young men, perpetrators of much crime, are also its main victims. It is also now known that England has a lower juvenile crime rate than many other European countries. But the media are wedded to the image of the yob because it seems to encapsulate the real and imaginary fears of our times. It may be that the yob is carrying the weight of a masculinity which, for a variety of reasons, middle-class society finds increasingly unacceptable, and rhetorically dumps on to the men of the lower class. He is a classic scapegoat, lugging around the sins of our culture. Young men, perhaps the most vulnerable members of society, are targeted as its main problems. The worry is that feminism's cultural influence has made this possible, either directly or in the reaction it creates which has ensured that the problem is seen in gender terms: testosterone is the problem – or the absent father.

The changing role of fathers is another area where old-fashioned feminism has shown itself to be at best, inadequate and at worst, damaging. As with concerns over young men's criminal behaviour, men's anxieties about their role in the family have fuelled the idea of a male crisis. However, suggestions of a real crisis have been dismissed by many feminists with a reassertion of female rights and male inadequacies. As a result, the discussion of fathering has been the source of some of the most antagonistic exchanges between women and men, and little progress has been made in helping ordinary individuals make sense of, and enjoy the changes.

The fact that the role of the father is being debated at all is symptomatic of just how extensive social changes have been. It is not a discussion confined to family experts, social theorists or commentators on gender behaviour; it is everywhere. In recent years journalists have produced acres of newsprint on the subject of fatherhood: how to be a good father, the joys of being a father, and the sufferings of being a son. The underlying preoccupation is with doubts and uncertainties. 'Once the baby has appeared the degree to which the man should be involved has yet to be decided upon,' writes Jim White in the *Independent* (27 April 1996). 'In the past it was easy: he wasn't. Now no one is quite sure. There is no standard role model'. The tone of these debates is summed up in an article, 'Daddy's Home': 'A lot of men want to do things differently from their own fathers. But they don't know what to do instead. There's a loss of confidence and nerve' (London City Airport Magazine, 1996).

While this debate about a father's role shows up all the male uncertainties typical of our times, it also reveals something else: the open hostility with which some feminists greet men's attempts to change. On this subject more than on almost any other, feminists have insisted that men's self-consciousness and anxieties about their role are actually anxieties about lost status, signs of the backlash, and attempts to hang on to the powers of the father which feminists so hated. Anyone who sympathizes with men's anxieties on this score is likely to be branded as suffering from nostalgia for the patriarch. I know this to my cost, having broached the subject in the *Guardian* only to be met with considerable anger from certain feminists. Yet, in spite of being accused of this nostalgia, I remain convinced that some of the contemporary gender shifts are throwing up real issues for men about how they live out their role as fathers. Some men are experiencing real difficulties around fatherhood, not just imaginary backlash ones, and these are of no necessary benefit to themselves or to their children unless women respond with greater magnanimity.

The loss of certainty around fathering is not altogether surprising. As with all other taken-for-granted male roles, fathering has come unstuck. The combination of social and economic transformations undermining the male breadwinner model, with feminism's demand that men abandon authoritarianism within the family, means that roles are much less clear. Many men welcome the end of the old expectations about fathering, especially when relationships are settled and going well. It's a small price to pay for greater intimacy and a more democratic family, which many feel their own fathers lost out on. As Lenny Henry puts it: 'I think being part of your child's upbringing is more important than anything. My dad was always at work, so I hardly saw him except in the evenings' (*You Magazine*, 15 June 1997). Alongside these positive feelings, however, there is a widespread loss of nerve and some of this has to be attributed to recent feminist stridency on this subject.

In the 1970s feminism had a relatively straightforward, if underdeveloped, attitude to fatherhood. Then feminists largely looked to men to be supportive, to involve themselves in the family to help women transform themselves. Now, as the transformation seems complete, the language has changed; some women are describing men's new position as not so much 'different' as 'redundant'. Yvonne Roberts, opening a debate in *She* magazine (September 1993) on 'Why Can't Men and Women Just be Friends', states: 'What women and men have to decide is exactly what, in the 1990s, is a father for.' Her question though typical is not dismissive. She answers that women should look to fathers to offer 'humane' involvement. This is more than can be said for other feminists. Bea Campbell, writing about hostility to single mothers in her book *Goliath*, seems to know the answer to Roberts' question: not a lot. She says: 'to reveal the redundancy of the men is the real crime of the mothers.' Sue Slipman, then director of the National Council for One Parent Families, was even more contemptuous. Responding to the complaint by right-wing theorist Charles Murray that single mothers are responsible for the social alienation of the new underclasses, she writes: 'He cannot explain why any woman in her right mind, should want to take one of his "new rabble" home' (*Sunday Times*, March 1992).

The defensive tone, while out of touch with what most women seem to want from their lives, is not exactly surprising. As this book has shown, social commentators of all political persuasions have pinned the social disintegration of the 1990s on fatherless families, that is single mothers: 'women who think it's their right to have several children by itinerant men and expect us to support them in perpetuity' (Lynda Lee Potter in *Daily Mail*). Many feminists have been forced to speak up on behalf of these scapegoated women, understanding only too well that single mothers rarely choose their condition. Typically, after a report, *Families without Fatherhood* (Institute of Economic Affairs, 1993), made grandiose claims about the cataclysmic consequences for fatherless families, Suzanne Moore joked: 'Having a father helps kids stop being poor, educationally retarded and delinquent. Apart from that, though, it remains unclear what fathers do that is so important' (*Guardian*, 17 September 1993).

In feminism's more buoyant days, when men's role in the family was regularly dismissed as little more than that of an unreliable dishwasher, most men would have taken such remarks on the chin. After all, there were centuries of men's scorn for women to redress. Those interested in social justice would have instantly recognized the need to challenge the old patriarchal assumptions about what a father should be. But the days of genial masochism are over. Now tossing around statements about the redundancy of fathers has become part of a rather more deadly sport between anti-feminist and feminist groupings contesting family policy in which, unfortunately, triumphalism and its reaction block real understanding.

Feminism's insistence that father's role is at best opaque and at worst redundant has been met by anger from the Men's Movement and its fellow-travellers. They take these 'jokes' as the real agenda of an ever-powerful group. Neil Lyndon's diatribe *No More Sex War: The Failures of Feminism* claims that the hidden agenda of feminism is 'the elimination of the father'. The UK Men's Movement, as we have seen, is certainly convinced that feminist rhetoric about paternal redundancy has become the literal aim of recent policy changes, caused by judicial kow-towing to feminism. No-fault divorces, they claim, achieve feminism's ultimate objective, allowing 'the wife to off-load her legally defenceless husband and children whenever she fancies a life-style change' (*Male View*, 1994).

Such views may seem paranoid and marginal but in the 1990s they were echoed by a whole range of far more respectable theorists who thought a society where the father was displaced was not just unfair on men but disastrous for the whole society. This certainly echoes Charles Murray's idea that increasing numbers of single mothers means increasing numbers of men without any investment in the community. Robert Bly talks of these young men as perpetual adolescents, unable to take an adult place in society. David Blenkenhorn takes it further in *Fatherless America* (1997); the reason why the apparent displacement of the father is so serious is that, without it, there is nothing to channel men's aggressive and anti-social impulses. Melanie Phillips agrees with him. 'Male breadwinning ... is neither arbitrary or anachronistic,' she says:

> it is important to cement masculine identity and civilise male aggression. That is why unemployment has played havoc with young boys' socialisation and shattered their fathers' emotional and physical health. Employment is an instrumental goal given activity which permits men to serve their families through competition. It directs male aggression into pro-social purposes. That is why employment is a fundamental means of integrating men into family life. (*The Sex Change State*, 1997)

For the marginal Men's Movement, this sudden welter of sociological concern about how the father's role had been undermined came just in time. Feminism's marginalization of men would have been all but complete, declares their journal *Male View*, were it not for the fact that people are finally beginning to notice the terrible effects of paternal redundancy on children, children's behaviour and social cohesion:

> greater than all other threats to feminism, is the emerging truth that the primordial matriarchy, the widespread lone-mother 'family', generated by the divorce law and the welfare system, is not an 'alternative lifestyle' but a pre-civilised reproductive unit, appropriate to the pigsty and the rabbit warren, totally incapable of sustaining civilisation and increasingly recognised as a principal source of many forms of social pathology. (*Male View*, April 1995)

From the mid-1980s the displacement of the father had begun to feature in political discourse too. Influenced by Charles Murray, several ministers during the John Major years publicly expressed the fear that without coercion to marry, the basis for shared civilized values would crumble. Men would not only evade financial responsibilities but would float free of shared social values and drift into crime and anti-social behaviour. In other words, the family man, concerned to provide for his family, is seen as the fundamental basis of civilized society.

In July 1993, Cabinet minister John Redwood described the increase in single mothers as 'one of the greatest social problems of our day'. He talked not only about the need to make men pay for their children (a process set in motion in a haphazard and largely unsuccessful way by creation of the Child Support Agency, supposedly to pursue deserting fathers), but also about the need to restore them to the home to offer 'the normal love and support that fathers have offered down the ages'. His comments were followed by a succession of ministerial statements following his lead in blaming the increase in fatherless families on the church, or on 'politically correct ideas', especially feminism, for encouraging the idea that bringing up a child alone is all right. In 1996, John Bowles, a junior Cabinet minister, repeated these views while calling on single mothers to give up their children for adoption. Blair's New Labour government, while avoiding some of the explicit hostility to single mothers, seemed to share the previous government's concern with the damaging effects of the disintegrated family.

Most discussions of the role of the father and the effect on this of women's changed status are overwhelmed by the weight of this apocalyptic language. It has been hard to think about, let alone pursue in a clear-headed way, what has really been happening, why exactly fathers are confused about their role, whether or not this is a bad thing and especially whether feminism is in any way responsible for these changes.

There are some who deny that feminism has had anything to do with the increase in single mothers. Instead, wider changes in family structures are held responsible. Some feminists invert the argument: men are entirely responsible. Using the flip-side of the right-wing argument, they say that without the constraints of traditionalism men are showing their true colours and abandoning women. Having been abandoned in this way, women have had to cope and, so the argument runs, done so well that they really have exposed male redundancy.

Feminists are wrong to deny that their philosophies had no

significant impact on the increase in single parents. Women's refusal to be stigmatized by pregnancy outside marriage, women's insistence on their financial independence (meaning that divorce can be survived), and women's insistence that they can work and look after children have all contributed to a climate where single parenthood is not viewed always as a disaster but sometimes as a viable option. Polly Toynbee, an apologist for Harriet Harman's drive to get single mothers off benefit and into work, constantly returns to the theme that the only thing that will really help poorer women is for them to become breadwinners themselves.

Feminist ideology, however, has been only one part of a much wider change. Changes affecting the family started at the end of the nineteenth century, long before the economic revolution traced in the early chapters of this book. The patriarchal family, as various historians have pointed out, was in fact a middle-class ideal; it is disputable whether it ever extended across all classes even in its so-called heyday. The English poor have always had a reputation for being sexually somewhat ungovernable. Victorian philanthropy, as I have already mentioned, was full of concern about the sexual promiscuity and the immorality of 'the lower orders', and showed a marked desire to pull working-class men into the model of middle-class paternal responsibility.

At the beginning of the nineteenth century at least, there was fairly widespread consensus that the ideal form of the family was that achieved by the middle classes where the father had apparently sacred and natural rights over his wife and children. By the end of that century a series of reforms had already begun to extend the legal rights of wives, mothers and children. From the 1920s onwards, childcare manuals increasingly stressed the centrality and importance of the mother in the welfare of her children, something which immediately began to problematize the paternal role. By the 1960s, the transformations were virtually complete. The patriarchal model had been replaced by a more democratic model: the family was a unit of equals in which each person had rights, and the welfare of the children was paramount.

Given the fact that the origin of these changes dates back some time, it is perhaps surprising that it has only been in the 1990s that various men's groups and fathers' groups have started mourning their lost status as if it is a new development. If the changes began so long ago, there should have been plenty of time to acclimatize to this more democratic and companionate model of the family. In reality, even though the legal *ideals* of the family had already changed by the mid-twentieth century, the actual workings of the law continued to assume that a father's role entitled him to power and authority, based on a gendered division of labour. The father was assumed to be the economic provider and the mother the one to care for the children. Many legal decisions were made on the grounds that it would be 'ridiculous' for a man to stay at home looking after children when he could command more than the woman at the workplace. In assuming that the father was the economic provider, the law also assumed that the father had certain claims to power, authority and dominance, particularly in the areas of discipline, moral authority and financial control. In other words, the main way in which the law continued to construct paternal subjectivity was through reference to a man's capacity for paid employment to provide for the family, not because of any number of other things he might do for his children.

We have already seen that the actual economic role which was assumed in this legal model has been taken away from men by more recent economic changes. On one side, these economic changes have made the provider role much more uncertain for men. Even when they want it, it is not always available. Certainly, given the restructuring of the economy, it is a much less stable and reliable source of identity. Simultaneously, modern women have been challenging this role of economic provider precisely because they rejected the authority and dominance which it gave men both inside and outside the family. Thus, changes which were already under way now were given prominence in political and social debate and in general public awareness.

Importantly, the role of the decent family man who provided

for his family neither required nor presupposed any other connection with his children. If anything, it presupposed an absent, working father. So long as he provided for his family, he could call himself a good father, however little he involved himself emotionally. Not surprisingly, then, as the role of economic provider secure within the family unit breaks down, some men who have not forged other ways of connecting with their families have been left feeling adrift. It is no coincidence that the most aggrieved and vituperative tones come from men active in the Men's Movement who are worried about how far economic and legislative changes have encouraged female autonomy. They see the breakdown of traditional masculine authority within the family not just as synonymous with the breakdown of the family itself, but also with the end of their connectedness to the family.

This is the same complaint which has been heard from the Campaign for Justice in Divorce in the 1970s right through to the more organized and effective Families Need Fathers in the 1990s. Some of the people involved in these groups seem bitter that economic changes and the law have made it possible for families to dispense with fathers altogether, as if men's financial contributions were the essence of their fathering. Recently, their complaints have struck a much more resonant note, mainly because of new ideologies about the psychological need for men to be involved with their children.

One of the principal ways in which traditionalists have tried to secure their dominance within the family as the old patriarchal rights have broken down has been through a psychological discourse about the need for male role models. This has been a powerful element in fanning hostility to fatherless families which are seen as psychologically unhealthy. All the symptoms of an increasing sense of social divisiveness and the breakdown of any attempts at community provision, in particular the symptoms of urban unrest and crime, are now laid at the door of this psychologically malfunctioning unit. Traditionalists are particularly concerned about the absence of male discipline and authority.

Ironically, feminism has unintentionally strengthened this

discourse in two ways. First, as we have seen, feminism has forced a degree of self-consciousness on men about their masculinity. Paradoxically, though intended to radicalize men, this has allowed certain men to think of masculinity as something which needs to be passed from man to man, from father to son, something which a boy needs to be exposed to directly in order to understand it. Second, as we have seen in the previous chapter, one feminist tendency has been to insist that crime should be understood as a 'male' problem. This has been latched on to as further evidence of what happens to boys who have not directly experienced older role models. This, as we have seen, enabled Robert Bly and the new masculinists to lay the blame for gang culture and social disintegration on the absence of any process of male initiation.

So far I have outlined these theories without challenging them, but do these gloomy scenarios painted about fatherhood have any basis? It needs to be said at once that they are built on a morass of unproven assumptions and muddled thinking. The absent father has been a recurrent theme through history; there have been many periods when, either through death or war, men were absent from the family. Ever since industrialization the urban working class has shown consistently much less enthusiasm for the traditional married unit than the middle classes; periods of social unrest have tended to reflect economic changes more than changes in family patterns. In addition, the 'provider' father could be accused of having been absent in other crucial ways, emotionally and psychologically. As academic Charlie Lewis has put it: 'The paradox of patriarchy is that, while a father may be head of his family, he is constrained from being a central character in it' (quoted in *You*, 15 June 1997). Finally, there is a need to set the record straight about single mothers, for the notion of the single mother choosing her solitude and remaining in it is profoundly misleading; only a tiny minority choose single motherhood, even teenage girls appear to believe that boyfriends will stay when the baby is born. Many enter into other stable unions later.

These, of course, the usual feminist refutations of the idea that the displacement of the father is responsible for social disintegration. But while I agree with all these points, somehow in the course of exchanges about the construction of fatherhood, about the evidence of history and the need to treat statistics with caution, important questions are lost. Positions are polarized between the fathers' rights lobby wanting a return to a traditional role because it is difficult to imagine any other secure connection to children, and the vocal feminist position which asserts that 'we might as well get on without them'. Left out of this is any recognition that men really may feel a need to affirm a secure connection with their children without returning to the past.

When relationships between men and women and their children are working well, the gains of greater intimacy obviously far outweigh any losses, and few men stop to question the paternal role. 'I have longed for children for so long,' says actor Tom Cruise. 'They come before everything, before career, films, business – everything. Being a father has made me ecstatically happy.' Most men have evolved new roles without looking for labels. 'I'm a hands-on kind of a dad,' says another actor, Pierce Brosnan. 'I've got it down to a fine art. When Dylan wakes up in the night, its automatic – out of bed, have everything lined up: a little water, napkins to clean him off, new nappies.' (Quoted in *You*, 15 June 1997.)

When relationships break down, though, some men realize they have been playing a marginal role, a walk-on part to the central drama. Women may have been working but few have given up their central role with the child or delegated primary care of their children to their partners. They've been adding roles to the point where men have begun to wonder if there's anything left for them to do. As Adrian Mourby puts it when writing about his son's impression of domestic life:

For John the serious business of parenting is done by my wife who, like many women of her generation, has managed to devote herself simultaneously to her career, housework and childcare while bringing seemingly inexhaustible supplies of love and patience to all three roles. Daddy by comparison is someone who is around less often, who demands silence when he is working and who clearly functions as Mum's deputy in the running of our domestic life. (*Guardian*, 7 January 1998)

When a family relationship hits difficulties, fathers may suddenly find themselves without a role and without the language to describe their relationships with children. The only place where these feelings have been given a voice has been in the right-wing, pro-family lobby which has vociferously pointed out that 90 per cent of all divorces end in women gaining custody of all children, and men being granted 'visitation' rights.

Is there really nothing one can say about the positive attributes of fatherhood without being accused of criticizing single mothers, discriminating against children whose fathers are absent, or feeding the right-wing pro-traditional family lobby? Any statement about the positive role of fathers runs this risk. In one of the most interesting contributions on this subject, *The Good Enough Parent of Either Sex* (1995), psychoanalyst Andrew Samuels explores what it is a father can bring to the family without resorting to traditional authoritarian roles, yet he feels compelled to add 'of Either Sex' just in case it should be construed that he thinks only men can perform this role.

The most interesting work about fatherhood so far has come from psychoanalysts and psychotherapists like Samuels. They have dared say (although heavily qualifying these statements) that, in their clinical experience, children of divorced parents experience problems. Sebastian Kraemer of the Tavistock Clinic writes:

The absence of fathers is largely due to parental separation, which in about 90% of cases results in living with the mother. About a third of these children lose all contact with their fathers often because access is upsetting. Children from families in which the parents have separated are over-represented in child mental health clinics. Even after allowing for the effects of social class and intellectual ability, there is evidence of the independent long-term effects of family disruption – earlier marriage/cohabitation, earlier parenthood, and poor academic performance. (*Active Fathering for the Future*, 1995)

Of course, these consequences are not necessarily as cata-strophic as he suggests, but they are still brave words, especially as he goes on to say that he has never yet met a child who did not wish he or she was part of an ordinary two-parent family, however understanding and realistic they are about their parents' reasons for divorce. Kraemer is highly critical of the old patriarchal model of the family with the emotionally distant provider father, so he has no nostalgia for lost paternal rights. Instead, he is interested in the advantages brought by active fathers, that is fathers prepared to help with the childcare and involve themselves in intimate relationships with children.

Kraemer cites evidence that children of fathers who share more than 40 per cent of their care, 'demonstrate more cogni-tive competence, increased empathy, less sex-stereotyped beliefs and a more internal locus of control' (ibid.). With two parents involved, children experience a greater richness of care-taking, experiencing different ways of connecting which they can see often don't fit the sexual stereotypes from the media. Two parents can also make up for each other's defects. He also cites as an advantage that the child is able to witness another relationship, thus developing his or her capacity to understand others: 'If the link between the parents perceived in love and hate can be rated in the child's mind, it provides him with a prototype for an object relationship of a third kind in which he is not a participant.'

Of course, all this could be provided by someone of the same sex or a step-parent, hence Andrew Samuels's anxiety not to appear to be discriminating against alternative family arrangements. Nevertheless, he is still prepared to push the boat out about a father's relationship with his child. An active and physically affectionate father can bring to a son a feeling of 'homosociality', an ability to relate to other men affectionately and communally rather than in constant flight away from homosexuality. More radically, Samuels suggests that a father's affection for his daughter can break up an identification with motherhood, introducing her to the possibility of imagining and finding her way between many roles which he describes as 'a key social issue for women'. He talks about the affirmation which a father can give to his daughter as an evolving sexual being. Like Kraemer, Samuels insists this is not an abusers' charter; he cites evidence that fathers who are closely involved with their children's care from an early stage are less likely to sexually abuse their children.

The degree to which some feminists will simply rule out such discussions was made clear to me by Bea Campbell's response when I mentioned Samuels's ideas about father–daughter relationships in a newspaper article. She replied: 'Samuels, she says, proposes that the father (but not the mother presumably) can affirm "his daughter as an evolving, sexual being". Spooky' (*Guardian*, 15 April 1995). To mention that a sexual affirmation might be a dynamic in father–daughter relationships is *not* in and of itself spooky; it would be spooky only if the father were to *abuse* his daughter's sexuality, not if he noticed it. And to pretend that any man who talks about a father's physical relationship with a child is sinister is just a way of slamming the door on a difficult area of discussion.

In fact, writers such as Kraemer and Samuels are merely attempting to open up a more positive consideration of the father within the family. These are not prescriptions; they are only putting into words what the majority of democratically-inclined fathers are already unconsciously acting on. Part of the problem is that men don't really have a language for the many new roles that they are already playing in the family; they do not have the words to describe what it is they are doing when they care for a newborn baby, as many of them already do, or to describe the ways in which they feel protective towards their children.

Women have become lazy about using the word 'maternal' to describe all those aspects of care and nurturing which go on in the family. And feminists have seized on the hegemony women have over these maternal qualities, exploiting the idea of a special bond which develops between a mother and child. As Kraemer says: 'This romanticism belies the fact that the male's competence in and contribution to, child-rearing is potentially very similar to the female's.' Certainly, if some women were prepared to be a bit more honest about the less pleasant attributes hidden under the term mothering, that romanticism might be more difficult to sustain and we might be able to hear more about modern fathering.

When I sat down to write this chapter, I happened to hear an item on BBC Radio 4's 'From Our Own Correspondent'. The item was called 'Letter to Daniel' and was written by foreign correspondent Fergal Keane to his newborn son. This was an extraordinary and powerful description of his emotions when Daniel was born in Hong Kong, something he wanted his child to know when older. He described lying close to the newborn baby experiencing deep feelings of tenderness towards humanity, unable to prevent the memories of all the children he had seen suffering or dying in the course of his travels. He was astonished by his fierce desire to protect his own child and by his feelings of loss about his own father, an alcoholic who died alone. He couldn't help the thought that in his own child's cry he heard the 'distinct voice of family, the voice of hope'.

This rawness, this sense of connectedness with humanity, with simultaneous grief and hope, are emotions not unfamiliar to women. This is the language often used to describe the powerful emotions felt when becoming a mother, but we are not so accustomed to hearing such descriptions from men, especially from men who do the 'hard' jobs requiring traditional 'male' emotional distance and objectivity. Left to talk about his feelings for his own son, though, Fergal Keane gave voice to what many obviously feel about the intensity and complications of a father's love. So what should we call the emotions which he describes? Are they maternal because more often described by mothers or are they paternal? If they are, how do paternal feelings differ from maternal ones? It stuck me that Fergal Keane has no lack of confidence about how to be a father in a less traditional way, but as a society we lack the language to reflect this non-stereotypical response.

Perhaps if Fergal Keane had been asked what was his role as a father in the 1990s, all that extraordinary clarity and connectedness would have been lost. Perhaps, like so many men now, he would have groped to define his role by a series of negatives – not to be absent for his own child, not to be an authoritarian and distant father like his own. Perhaps if he had been asked to list the positives, he too would have displayed the diffidence and loss of nerve which we so often hear is characteristic of contemporary fathering.

Maybe women are unwilling to let men inhabit this space, fearing that if men enter this most significant bond, women will have nothing left. This may be why women, in spite of demanding changes from men, have been reluctant to give them a more central role, wanting them to shop and cook, unload the buggy and sterilize the bottles rather than to share in the primary and intimate bond with the child.

Certainly this seems to be the implication of Bea Campbell's response to my suggestion that we should allow men in more and encourage them to evolve a language about fathering. Their journey to transform the fathering role, in reaction to their own fathers, is just as significant as the impetus which produced feminism when women decided they did not want to behave like their mothers' generation. Campbell dismisses these thoughts as ignoring the fact that, when asked to show themselves as present in the family, men have simply bunked off: 'What feminists like women in general have longed for from fathers is something so simple and elusive – co-operation.' But that precisely sums up what I am talking about: the only role assigned to men is to support the greater bond of mother and child. Ironically, given that the demand for support is couched in terms of feminism's demand for men to come fully on board, it may be the very reason why men find it so easy to leave.

When I was writing my previous book, *Our Treacherous Hearts*, I had noticed women's reluctance to hand over more of the mothering role to fathers. The women I interviewed for that book at the beginning of the 1990s were, for the most part, mothers of young children. Most had worked, at least until they became mothers, and many were still attempting to combine motherhood with work outside the home, albeit often in a reduced way. These women were in many way typical of our image of contemporary women – expecting to continue working while they had children or hoping to return to work at some point.

Importantly, they were also women who felt all ambivalences identified by feminism as the 'problems' of 1990s' mothering. They often felt guilty, sometimes for working and leaving their children in someone else's care, sometimes for not working and being dependent on their husbands' income; the latter made them feel 'less interesting' as women in the world. Almost all were united in speaking eloquently of the pressures they experienced in their lives because most still took on the larger part of domestic responsibilities, and were left feeling exhausted and overstretched.

Yet in spite of these 'problems', I was unable to conclude that what these women were experiencing were simply the external pressures of a society which does not make it easy for the working mother. It was difficult to reduce what I was hearing to the standard feminist interpretation that women are forced to perform 'the second shift' or to carry 'the double burden' because men are ducking their responsibilities. Instead, I became convinced that women themselves still desperately want to hang on to that central role in their children's lives. This was an incredibly potent feeling. Many women would prefer to give up a job altogether, or to risk slipping off a career track by reducing their hours, or to exhaust themselves by trying to act as a full-time mother while actually being a full-time worker – anything rather than lose that feeling of centrality to their children's lives.

What was remarkable about these interviews was just how many, for whatever reason, felt not only that they did not share full responsibility with their partners but that, at some profound level, they did not want to. Maybe I had unconsciously been looking for this evidence when I started the book. I had been taken aback by my own possessive response to mothering. Before the birth of the baby, my partner and I had concocted all sorts of fanciful and impractical schemes about how we would share looking after the baby. When the child was born, I quite simply didn't want to let go. It was much easier to let go of a conventional career structure, changing the pattern of my work to fit around the child. The research for my book confirmed I was not alone.

There seemed to be profound reasons why, when it came to it, in spite of the welter of opportunities, so many women chose the traditional path. It was hard to miss, for instance, just how many women of different ages and different class backgrounds would talk of the overpowering need to be needed, and the deep fulfilment of looking after a tiny dependant. At one end of the spectrum this was a simple pleasure at satisfying someone's needs and experiencing an incomparable love. Sometimes, though, it blurred into a more neurotic need for another's dependency. Looking after a dependant certainly gives life meaning; it fulfils something very deep when you are loved in an apparently unqualified way. But such feelings of wanting to be the centre of your child's life lead to extra burdens as well as having undoubted compensations.

More surprising, perhaps, was that many women with careers found that attending to these deeper needs 'solved' certain conflicts and discomfort which they had been feeling in their working lives. Ambivalence about the working world was at the forefront of reasons women gave me for downgrading their careers and sticking with traditional sex roles at home. Women found careers especially difficult when they entailed the competitive promotion of self against others, or involved aggression as a normal part of the working environment. I was surprised just how often women described a feeling of relief at dropping out of the working world (even if only temporarily) to concentrate on something which felt fundamentally both more important and more pleasant.

Of course, most of the women I talked to were determined to avoid burying themselves in the family – something which they saw as having frustrated and often depressed their mothers' generation. So it was also surprising to encounter the very high ideals of mothering which went with these contemporary decisions. No less than in the 1950s, '90s mothers seemed to be driven by potent ideals about good mothering, about what a mother should do and how a child should turn out. In the 1960s and '70s feminism had included a critique of women for pouring so many of their own hopes and expectations into their children. Maternal altruism, self-denial and identification with children were criticized as limiting the lives of housewives and mothers. Feminists are often accused of idealizing work; if they did, it was partly because of this belief that women should stop living vicariously through their children and find fulfilment for themselves.

Yet although work itself has become more commonplace among mothers, women still seem to sublimate their own hopes, ambitions and competitiveness into their children and partners. I was astonished at just how weighty a business modern mothering had become. Instead of lightly shrugging off the oppressive mantle of over-identified motherhood, we seem to have added yet more layers. Indeed, in many ways, mothers of the 1980s seemed to be pursuing ever more demanding ideals about what mothering should involve and what could be expected of their children have become ever more demanding

– clubs for this and that, accelerated learning, endless stimu-
lation to ensure high achievement.

Competitiveness eschewed at work in favour of more 'feminine' priorities was not always successfully banished. It often
seemed to come back with a vengeance around women's hopes
for their children. The assertiveness and aggressiveness which
discomforted us at work was permitted, positively encouraged
sometimes, in our partners and male children. I called the book
Our Treacherous Hearts not because I thought women who gave
up work in order to stay at home were letting down 'the sisters',
but rather because I saw women colluding in a process by which
they attempted to hold at bay certain difficult or unacceptable
feelings, such as competitiveness and aggression, by pushing
them on to men or children. I lost count of the number of
times women told me about their partner's need for success or
rather proudly how their sons couldn't be held back from their
natural assertiveness.

In many ways it was a very old story only in a modern guise
– a splitting of attributes between men and women so that men
and boys had to carry competitiveness, aggression and so on. I
was not condemning what I saw – on the contrary, I recognized
much of it in myself. And in some ways the decisions women
were taking seemed to contain a vision of the future, namely
the importance of combining work and family and not letting
work corrode human needs and relationships. But there was
also complicity in not acknowledging the role women play in
constructing the men, and upholding the division of labour in
the home, which in the next breath they might claim oppresses
them. And there was certainly complicity involved in imagining
women to be somehow more virtuous and superior than men.

I am occasionally asked whether the findings in *Our Treacherous Hearts* will stand the test of time, or whether they are just
a vignette of a particular historical moment. Maybe, it is suggested, the emotions and conflicts which I describe were the
result of women not having enough role models ahead of them.
Perhaps now with more and more women entering the labour
force, the decisions are changing. Obviously, as working

mothers have become the norm, as workplaces introduce enabling facilities and policies, and with a new government making the lot of working mothers a top priority, then cultural expectations are shifting significantly. The women I interviewed were really the first generation inheriting expectations that they *should* continue working as mothers so perhaps it was not all that surprising that their attitudes lagged behind.

There had also been some very specific social and political forces at work through the 1980s which may have shaped women's responses. This was a time of widening opportunities but it was also a time of confusion and difficulty. Very rapidly Britain had gone from being a society where women who worked outside the home were considered neglectful, to a society where it was acceptable, even desirable. Feminism, the economy and aspirations based on the dual-income family had created these changes, but there was no support from the state and political culture to aid these changes. The Conservative government was at best ambivalent and at worst hostile to working mothers; muddled messages were the order of the day. Margaret Thatcher's own comments about working and mothering summed it up; she could manage her career but only because she had a 'treasure' at home to look after the twins and run the house. The implicit message was that it was acceptable for women to work so long as this remained a private decision and did not alter the state's official relation to men and women workers or childcare provision.

This abdication of any responsibility on the part of the state to regulate and provide for new working patterns was typical of other social changes which made mothering seem so onerous. Many responsibilities which might previously have rested with the state were pushed back on to the individual. The political and ideological thrust of the time was to shift provision away from the 'nanny state' so hated by Thatcher to individuals taking more responsibility for their families: private health insurance, private pensions, more parental responsibility for children's education, personal responsibility for health. On the educational front, what started with calls for parents to involve themselves more in their children's education and the running of schools soon became an all-out attack on the competencies of state provision. Into that anxious space much pressure fell on mothers to take increased responsibility in parenting.

There was also a general deterioration in aspects of life which had a direct impact on families. Mothers bringing up children throughout that period were the first really to experience a society where certain taken-for-granted lifestyles disappeared. The increase in road traffic, awareness of child murders, a general increase in levels of crime and violence and new attention paid to the phenomenon of bullying – all these contributed to the emergence of a society where it felt unacceptable to leave young children unsupervised. It was no longer possible to walk to school unaccompanied as I did from the age of five. You can gauge precisely how anxious parents had become from proposals made by some parents at the time that children should not actually have playtime in the open playground at school because of fears of bullying.

Attributing immense psychological importance to mothering was not new. The gurus of each decade since the Second World War – John Bowlby in the 1950s, Benjamin Spock in the 1960s, Penelope Leach in the 1980s – all emphasized the absolutely central role of the mother's relationship with the child. This would determine, they said, not just the physical survival of the child but its ultimate well-being and psychic health. By the 1980s, in the context of growing concern about moral decline and children's behaviour, the parental (maternal) bond had never seemed more important. Whereas Bowlby demanded only that a mother should be present to provide security, contemporary 'good mothering' involves educating, stimulating, organizing a complex social life, choosing the right education and attending to all the nuances of a child's psychological behaviour.

These social and political pressures certainly contextualize the experience of mothering which I encountered during my interviews, but they don't exhaust it. On the contrary, up-to-the-minute research confirms my sense that women themselves are

167

active in hanging on to their central role in the family and even in colluding with pushing on to men some of the traditional male attributes. In 1993 an academic, Dr Catherine Hakim, published research which seemed to bear out some of my less systematic findings (see Bibliography). Her more statistically-based research found that only a quarter to a third of mothers wanted careers and most found the option of part-time work attractive. Equal numbers stated they were happy to devote their lives to children. Her research confirmed that it was not expensive and inadequate childcare keeping women out of the workforce, but viewing work as of secondary importance to the family.

Hakim's aim was to challenge what she called feminism's great myths about work, claiming that feminists have promoted the idea that all women are desperate to work only because they themselves are desperate for high-powered careers. This, however, is not what is wanted by 'ordinary' women. She concludes that many of the directions of policy and legislation to make things easier for the working mother are of little relevance to those for whom the home is still number one priority. Hakim was accused by fellow sociologists of focusing on a group of women at a particular moment of their lives. Had she done her research vertically, it was said, interviewing the same women at different points in their lives, she might have elicited very different reactions.

> Today's contented housewife [Maureen Freely pointed out in the *Guardian* (1996), could be] tomorrow's single mother. Even if she remains happily married, she could find next week her husband has been made redundant. She might raise her children to believe a woman's place is in the home, but if her daughter goes to university, then that daughter is likely to reconsider. If she gets married and has children she will probably have to come up with a new compromise, and then another one, and another.

In other words, decisions for women about motherhood, work and the family were changing frequently and were hard to encapsulate in a single response. Although my book had included a wider range of ages, I also had this criticism levelled at my conclusion. Journalist Ann McFerran wondered whether the emotions which I described largely belonged to women who were looking after very young children. Some of the guilt and anxiety, at least about working, lessened as the children became older (interview with author).

Yet it is hard not to conclude that, however you look at it, however much these feelings intensify and lessen at different historical moments or at different times in your life, they remain centrally important in women's response to mothering. There is no evidence at all that the kind of decisions I described women struggling to make in *Our Treacherous Hearts* have become irrelevant. When more recently I wrote an article (*Guardian*, October 1997) criticizing the Labour Party's apparent over-idealization of work at the expense of full-time mothering in their plans to get single mothers back to work, I received many letters in agreement. It was clear that it is not just a lack of practical help which keeps women at home but other more complex feelings about a child's and a mother's needs. 'It's become a dangerous heresy in these New Labour times to argue the legitimacy of anyone staying at home to bring up children even for a short period,' says Melissa Benn, author of *Madonna and Child* (1997), 'but millions of middle-class women do it because they can; they have a breadwinning husband and so, more choices.'

No less than in the 1980s, the 1990s have been witness to a steady stream of high-profile women publicly renouncing working pressures to focus on home life. Maeve Haran, author of *Having It All* (1991), was the first high-profile woman to go, but there has been a steady stream since, including Coca-Cola boss Brenda Barnes, and several magazine editors, Linda Kelsey of *She* and Tina Gaudoin of *Frank*. Kelsey resigned under pressure of work and a desire to spend more time with her family. *She* had successfully targeted working mothers throughout the 1980s; its catchphrase had been 'For the women who juggle their lives', and Kelsey herself had seemed the emblem of the

169

generation for whom these new roles were easy. The *Mail on Sunday* commented: 'Like many women, Linda has discovered that having a child supersedes all other career choices . . . Most of us are left with a straight choice between career and motherhood if we want to do either really well. Because whatever the glossies tell you, juggling is balls.'

Nicola Horlick's book *Can You Have It All?* provoked the same debate. Having come to public attention accused of poaching staff from a City bank, millionaire Horlicks offered herself as the definitive proof that the '90s woman could combine mothering and work entirely successfully.

Horlick's account of her life nevertheless horrified many '90s women who found her version of motherhood chilling, Anne Robinson asked: how can Horlick claim to be a successful mother when we don't know the final outcome? 'She should wait until her offspring are in their thirties and she is satisfied none of them is sitting in therapy or a rehab clinic moaning: "if you had a mother like mine"' (The *Daily Express*, 19 September 1997). The death of her child from leukemia in 1998 removed the mask; there was no such thing as a woman exempt from the dilemmas and conflicts raised by being a working mother.

These comments are important because they expose what is a central element for women taking decisions about how to get the right balance between working and motherhood, an element often overlooked by feminists convinced that work is of overwhelming significance for women. This is not the case. When it is no longer a question of financial survival, working is no longer anything like as important as the issue of 'getting it right' around your children. Conspiracy theorists would love to see the strengthening of this psychological discourse as a conspiracy to undermine women's new-found position in the economy, but it is more complex than that. The great majority have accepted that it is possible to combine work and mothering in some form, but what is of overwhelmingly importance is the need individuals feel to do it right around the children. That is why there is so much desire for tangible proof that children are OK. That is why there is so much anxiety about children's behaviour and abilities as these are seen as proof that your personal decisions about the relative values of work and home are the right ones.

The child has become the pitch on which women's difficult decisions are played out, with the accomplished, early-developing child seen as the proof of doing it right. That is why there has been such an emphasis placed on 'hothousing', early learning and so on – as if educational and academic achievement were proof that all is well with a child. The issue for many women in the 1990s is not so much having-it-all as doing-it-right. In some, this manifests as anxiety, in others as fierce competition, and in others a general concern for the behaviour and morality of all children. Rather than these anxieties receding as women become more used to working, they have steadily increased since the end of the 1980s, for on top of the emphasis on achievement and behaviour have been laid fears about moral decline and crime, reaching out from 'the estates' right into the heart of middle-class homes through the transmission of mass media. What is clear in all these responses is that the battleground around the child which so characterizes contemporary society is partly created by the shifts in women's position over the last few decades.

Women who hang on to their traditional role in the family are not atypical backsliders. They reveal that the question of why traditional roles are upheld is much more complex than feminists would have us believe. Placing themselves so firmly at the centre of the family, women are clearly implicated not only in maintaining the traditional roles but also in the construction of masculinity. It's not just a question of women thwarted and oppressed, restrained from self-fulfilment, exploited by right-wing governments; there is a dialectic. Masculinity in its current forms relies on female expectations and vice-versa; they are part and parcel of the same story. This has implications for whether or not we accept the ways in which feminists have tried to problematize masculinity as some rogue response to economic crisis, as if women have nothing to do with all that.

The boy child has been the focus of the most pervasive worries of the last decade. His anti-social behaviour, his underachievement, his hopes for the future have all put him at the centre of escalating worries about masculinity, the family and parenting. Yet if ever we wanted an example of how much can be concealed by looking at social problems mainly in gender terms and using old-fashioned feminist assumptions, this is it. There is, packed into concern about the boy child, other more complex, less obvious elements: what is wrong with boys is not a problem of masculinity but a symptom of a new society with new interaction between the sexes.

The pathologizing of the yob as threatening to social order and cohesion had its roots in the divisive policies of the Tories as well as in the massive subterranean changes in family relations, but it did not shrivel and die along with Tory fortunes. By the mid-90s it was clear that a version of it – this time a pervasive worry about boys – formed a central plank in a new moral consensus willingly inherited by New Labour. Old liberal views on crime and poverty have gradually been replaced by a new focus on 'lack of morals' in which both the disintegrated family and anti-social masculinity are seen as prime causes. Yet, as with yobs, the problems incorporated into worries about boys cannot be reduced to gender.

The change in the moral consensus is easy to see if we compare how concern about disintegrating families was expressed in the mid-1990s and twenty years earlier. In 1974 Sir Keith Joseph had been forced to abandon his hopes for the Tory leadership after saying, 'our human stock is threatened by the rising proportion of children born to mothers least fitted to bring children into the world' (quoted in *Independent on Sunday*, 24 November 1993). Twenty years later no one turned a hair at suggestions that inadequate parenting is linked to social disintegration. The writing was clearly on the wall for the old liberal way of understanding crime by reference to poverty and disadvantage when, in 1992, two erstwhile left-wing sociologists, Norman Dennis and George Erdos, explained rioting in Tyneside not by reference to the usual explanation of poverty but as a result of the social disintegration brought about by fatherless families (*Fatherless Families*, Institute of Economic Affairs). By the time New Labour came to power, such views had widespread support.

Escalating anxiety about boys, especially the crimes and problems of ever younger boys has played a significant role in the formation of this new consciousness. Boy children were constantly in the news in the 1990s because of their involvement with crime on all levels. There have been bullies, uncontrollable schoolchildren, and even gang activities. Their ever younger ages proved that the core of society was rotten; children not even in their teens were charged with murder, rape, even manslaughter through reckless driving. If, as everyone agreed, children embody the future of society, boy trouble made the future look pretty bleak. This was a society no longer able to reproduce its values, or doing it so badly that it was cannibalizing itself. When the Ridings School in West Yorkshire was closed in 1996 it had become, according to reports, 'unmanageable': bullying was rife, one thirteen-year-old girl was pregnant, and truancy was commonplace. Reporters flocked there to interview the pupils and came back describing 'a chaotic war with violent pupils', a 'saga of indolence, incompetence, bullying' (*Daily Mail*, 25 October 1996).

Several high-profile crises concerning boys were critical here. One was the tragic killing of Jamie Bulger. In the acres of newsprint which followed, many tried to console themselves that at any time in history it wouldn't take much to tip bad boys into evil. But most agreed that the 'evil' unleashed in these boys was caused by the particular cocktail which is family life in contemporary society. 'Separated parents, poverty, truanting, videos, a brutal atmosphere', Geraldine Beddel summed it up in the *Independent* (24 November 1993). The particular fear was that this cocktail was a lethal brew for society's most difficult element – boys. Then came the incident which finally tipped the balance, bringing to the surface some of the latent issues at stake around these 'evil' boys. This was the stabbing of head-master Philip Lawrence, apparently by a member of a Triad-style gang in 1995. After this incident, even left-wing politicians were freely discussing what the right-wing press had dubbed 'this moral vacuum'. When Frances Lawrence, wife of the mur-dered headmaster, called on the public to join a movement dedicated to 'healing our fractured society, banishing violence, ensuring that the next generation are equipped to be good citizens and urgently debating how the moral climate can be changed for the better', she was talking to the converted. Most already endorsed her analysis. 'It is a savage irony', she said, 'that Philip whose values and examples did so much to guide children through the maze of immorality, became its victim' (*The Times*, 1996).

This vision of the good man destroyed by evil (or, as another newspaper put it, the 'tragic waste of the life of a good man for the worst reasons') tells much about precisely why boy children became such a focus of anxiety. Lawrence was killed by a boy who was part of a group with pretensions to being an actual criminal gang: 'The juvenile equivalent of Triad gangs', said the prosecutor, who 'wore black or dark clothes and bandannas or scarves over their faces, presumably to represent a uniform, command respect and instil fear.' His murder obviously there-fore raised the spectre of an increase in organized criminal gangs operating in our society. More frightening was the possi-bility that these boys were not so much hardened criminals as in some way typical; perhaps they just operated at the more extreme end of the kind of culture many boys were part, and this was now reaching out to destroy decent society.

Many commentators explicitly linked the killer's gang

with the tribal aspects of lad culture. What worried them was the male peer group apparently glorying in machismo culture, soaked in images of violence, whose notion of right extended only to wearing the right gear. When the tabloids described the gang's preoccupation with labels and the right gear, we were all meant to recognize what was being described: the shallow, consumerist, amorality culture of lad culture. 'Most of the gang wore jeans and T-shirts but Chindamo [the killer] wore more flamboyant baggies – baggy designer jeans and sweat shirts and expensive trainers' (*Daily Mail*, 18 October 1996).

This is more than decent society feeling physically threatened by the criminal culture of the yobs from the estate. This is a worry that through the pull of the peer group, yob culture threatens to reach out and destroy the very core of decent, middle-class society. In the male peer group, and in its extreme manifestation, the gang, the middle classes believe they can see the contagion spreading from the poorest right into middle-class society itself. Because there is an overlap of culture between the anti-social boy gang and the peer group culture of 'ordinary' boys, in a sexually unsettled society, the middle classes now feel contaminated as well. They worry about trashy videos, violent video games, expensive fashion worn by those who haven't earned the money, and peer group affiliation. In short, the boys are experienced as the moral weak link between the parent culture and social chaos.

Many middle-class parents live out a version of this struggle in their own families. Few are seriously worried that their sons might be members of a Triad-style gang, but many fret about their own child's acts of minor delinquency or their affiliations with the materialistic and hedonistic culture of drugs, clubbing and designer clothes. In a culture like ours – where in inner cities the children of the poor and marginalized mix closely with the affluent, and leisure drugs automatically bring some contact with criminality – the lines are by no means clear. The preoccupation of teenage boys with designer label shoes and clothes, their possession of the latest (violent) computer games, their need to sport the expensive strips of 'their' football clubs, their appetite for expensive venues, are often taken as signs of the shallow crassness of mass culture. 'Boys' ambitions', said recent research for Child Wise, 'are fuelled by TV cartoons, videos and electronic games while girls are said to adopt a more realistic attitude to school and the world' (quoted in *Daily Mail*, 6 February 1997).

From the boys' point of view, being seen to be part of these male peer group and feeling enhanced by that belonging is an absolutely integral part of how they form their adolescent masculine identity. Wearing the same clothes and doing the same stuff as the peer group is simultaneously an identification with strength and success and a talisman against vulnerability, the fear of being seen as different, as outside the group and therefore as a 'legitimate' target. It is not only a protection against the bad bullies out there, but also the dynamic by which bullying is created. As one of the Ridings School's violent bullies said in a newspaper interview, 'I do it to show off and because the others want me to. You've got to or you get bullied' (*Daily Mail*, 25 October 1996).

The essence of peer group affiliation is that it marks an allegiance to something far more potent than the home or school, hence the peculiar nonsense of governments' successive plans to give children lessons in morality. British primary schools have always been places where teachers have tried their hardest to teach society's basic morality. Yet by the time children reach their adolescence the pull of the peer groups is always stronger. A similar nonsense also infects most of the interpretations of *why* boys now perform so much worse academically than girls. Commentators interpret this as apathy brought on by the idleness and fecklessness spreading from the worst aspects of society, via peer group affiliation and mass culture, into all strata of society. It is this contamination which explains why boys do themselves such a disservice by not working hard like the girls.

In fact, it is the different prospects for boys and girls, and the different values placed on masculinity and femininity, which have skewed all that. Becoming a working woman seems like a valid goal in itself for girls. It doesn't even matter what job she does, her status will be enhanced just by becoming a working woman, something which is so highly rated in this society. Boys have to find a different source of self-evaluation and this has very little to do with the career paths predicted by performing well and achieving highly at school. This is because the moral status of masculinity, built on the foundation of hard work, a single career and the aim of providing for a family, has completely gone.

In an increasingly unpredictable economy, the main ways in which men and masculinity are visibly rated are connected with skills which have precisely nothing to do with the old values of paternal citizenship. The most obvious and visible ways for young men to acquire power, status and money have nothing to do with model male citizens which the new moralists constantly harp back to. It is skill, strength, music, looks and style – embodied in the adulation of footballers and pop groups – that count. Having certain attributes of laddish potency means that boys could almost be talent-scouted on the streets. Previously it was girls who, deprived of any pathway to achievement, dreamed of being plucked from the street by a model agency or a rich husband. Now it is boys who dream of being spotted on the football fields or forming the ultimate boy band.

These countervailing forces against accepting hard work, family devotion and the model of education, or apprenticeship, as the route to them are currently very strong indeed. Maybe if a boy has a good relationship with his father who in turn has a satisfying and equitable relationship with his partner, there is a fair chance the boy might see the advantages. Even so, especially through adolescence, other forces are stronger. Designer shoes and wear are marketed aggressively, using potent, stylish figures to reinforce their desirability. Instant wealth is not just seen as possible, but promised; it brings not family stability but sexual possibilities.

In the minds of the social commentators what has made current peer group affiliation seem so threatening is the high estimation of qualities associated with macho desperation – the assertion of physical strength and the use of courage and threat rather than legal means to obtain what is wanted. Boy gangs and acts of associated machismo 'delinquency' are by no means new, as suggested in the previous chapter. Even a recent survey of adult males of all classes revealed that 95 per cent had stolen or committed minor crimes in adolescence – a clear sign that, whatever the politicians might think, the law is not the same as morality. But machismo is a quality that is free to groups who feel threatened and otherwise disempowered, and if it is valued in particular boy peer groups, who have few alternatives, it does up the ante for all boys; be part of it or be threatened by it.

Of course, all these qualities which at first seem so contrary to mainstream values are not in fact so different. They are not so much out and out rejection as an unconscious rewriting of wider cultural preoccupations. The parents are wine snobs, the children drug-users; designer clothes on Cherie Blair are a sign of her stylishness, whereas expensive Nike trainers on boys are taken as a sign of their crass consumerism; the potency of the bully father becomes the machismo of street gangs; MPs bending the rules becomes street crime. Peer group affiliation forms a separate identity but echoes the deep values of the whole society.

There can be no doubt that this mirroring of the dominant culture, this rewriting but in a different modality with reference to other sources of identity, is one of the unconscious fears of those most concerned about boys' behaviour. Indeed, it is because of this threateningly close relationship with the parent culture that it becomes necessary to project all the negativity on to another, the alien, and, in the case of the right-wing press, the immigrant. The Philip Lawrence murder became such a potent symbol precisely because of this. What it offered was a vision of the source of the contamination as originally alien. In writing about Learco Chindamo, Lawrence's killer, and his mainly Filipino gang, the right-wing press presented him as the immigrant, dancing to a different moral master (his criminal father), brought up by his single, work-shy mother and all thoughtfully provided for by left-wing Camden Council. The contrast was particularly poignant in the portrait of the two sons of these families. Learco, school-shy, idolized his jailed Mafia father, writing him long admiring letters. Philip Lawrence's son was named Lucien, a 'bringer of light'. The pure boy versus the tainted, white versus black, the fathered boy and the fatherless boy.

I am not trying to belittle the significance of this murder or the terrible sense of despair it generated among those who saw a decent man destroyed by the very people he was trying to help. People were very shocked by it. If a teacher, one of the people we regard as a cornerstone of shared morality and authority (hence the Tory government and Ofsted's unseemly interest in them), could die in this way then there must be precious little left. But the actual event was also potent because it captured in a nutshell the latent perceptions of *why* this social disintegration is happening; that is, the threatening, fatherless immigrant boy with his crass consumerism undermining the values of the morally strong. One child pours out his adulation to a jailed murderer; the other writes to Santa Claus saying he wants nothing for Christmas, except the return of his father.

The real anxiety here is that the miasma of mass society – a culture without morality, without fathers, without authority – is reaching out to drag everyone down. Melanie Phillips describes a situation of 'social degradation ... of a startling absence of the most primitive instincts to care and nurture, of young men fathering babies indiscriminately ... of children growing up in unbridled savagery and lawlessness' (*Observer*, 17 October 1993). The concern around boys' and lads' culture is really concern about the pull of alien, anti-social values, the attraction of antagonistic peer groups for boys. The fear is that a continuum runs through lad culture, from the yobs and gangs of the estate, right into the heart of moral middle-class society. The obsession with winning boys back to 'social ties' by restoring the authority of church, family or school could also be seen as an attempt to wrest back authority from the 'alien' peer group, 'alien' understood either in terms of race or class (as embodied in the values of mass society – video games, videos, TV, designer labels, mass fashion). It is the moral weakness, the baseness, the anti-social nature of masculinity which is the dangerous gateway between an imagined other and decent, middle-class society.

This aspect of the crisis of masculinity is loaded down with other prejudices. Blaming everything on boys ought to make us suspicious. Boys are not by virtue of their sex weak, crass, consumerist, amoral; it's more that middle-class society feels deeply threatened by a new social landscape in which the old, rigid, comprehensible class and racial barriers are no longer standing. This is a new multi-cultural, post-feminist society where the old moral truths and old sources of authority have been shaken. Boys' peer group affiliations – formed at a time when uncomfortable gender changes are reinforcing boys' need for ways of affirming male identity – seem particularly unsettling. Blaming 'alien' groups is a way of drawing a line between respectability and those beyond the pale. Ironically, it has taken the murder of another Lawrence – Stephen – to unsettle the racist assumption that crime and danger are located in the 'alien' group.

There are very few social commentators who bother to look beyond the surface obsessions. Gender is accepted as the central explanation for 'the trouble with boys'. Again feminism and masculinist discourses re-inforce biological explanations of why our society is in so much trouble. At one conference (reported in *Independent on Sunday*, 24 November 1993), Christine McCaughey supported the feminist argument: 'Crime is incompatible with society's agenda for femininity and compatible with its agenda for masculinity. The traditional male-gender role encourages a preoccupation with status, success, competitiveness, impulsiveness, bravado, hedonism and contempt for qualities construed feminine.' Feminist Angela Phillips agreed: 'one factor is always closely correlated with criminality and that's the presence of the Y chromosome . . . Perhaps it's time we considered the possibility that in our society . . . there is something pathological about the way boys are raised.'

What Phillips identifies as pathological is the lack of any decent male roles in many boys' lives. Deserting and absent fathers are to blame: 'In the absence of close multi-dimensional male figures to learn from, that information must come from their peers. By the time they are seven, the coercive process of masculinization is well under way. Boys mercilessly tease those who do not conform to the group idea of masculinity.' This feminist explanation is echoed directly by masculinist explanations, although the latter locate the problem in not just the absence of men but also in the lack of authority which men have in those boys' lives. In *Sibling Society* (1997), Robert Bly describes the boy gang as the apotheosis of what's happening to the whole society. These boy gangs are the product of a society without intergenerational or vertical influences, that is fathers. They therefore cherish only the new, the immediate, and the horizontal and are driven by fashion and consumerism. Without proper role models in the family, the children learn from their peers. Doomed to remain proto-adults, they have no ritual of maturation. 'There is little in the sibling society to prevent a slide into primitivism, and into those regressions that fascism is so fond of.' In other words, all parties see boys as weak, immoral, crass, liable under pressure to regress into primitivism.

Whether they are feminists on the Left, underclass theorists on the Right or liberals such as Melanie Phillips, all seem to agree that without models of socially invested fathers, boys will degenerate. All share a strong conviction that there is something in the biological nature of masculinity pulling towards barbarism, away from civilization. If the model of fathering is breaking down, then boys will be attracted much more easily by corrupting, degrading, anti-social, alien values.

What's really at stake for these writers is fear of mass society and consumerism with its blurring of social lines, and resultant racial anxieties. But does that mean there is no real problem at all? Am I saying that boys have no case to answer? That their behaviour is neither better nor worse than it ever was? Certainly the great majority of people now seem to think there is a problem. Having cleared away some of the prejudices, though, we may have to understand the problem in different ways, which is not the same as saying we don't have a problem.

Even if we do not go along with the current level of hysteria, most people now acknowledge anxiety about how the next generation is being raised and the question of whether children (especially boys) are growing up detached from shared moral values. Most childcare professionals, however liberal, however wary of succumbing to hysterical and moralizing campaigns, all agree that they meet more disruptive children, more in conflict with the simple authority of schools, lashing out and causing misery not only to others but especially to themselves. 'If you listen to the people working in schools and clinics,' says Peter Wilson, director of the charity Young Minds, 'they are saying we are getting more and more families with multiple problems, with greater stress, showing more extreme behaviour, and more children who are less containable in the class room' (interview with author).

The important difference in his words is the concern for the suffering created for the individual children themselves. What worries teachers and childcare professionals, like Peter Wilson, is not the idea of the evil, amoral boy sliding into barbarism without the rule of the father, but the reality of vulnerable, unhappy children whose difficulties in accepting the authority of their parents (and the surrogate parents of school and law) will condemn them to a career of conflict, exclusion from school, lack of education and possibly a criminal career. These carers would be the first to recognize that although boys predominate, it is certainly not a problem exclusive to boys. Problems with discipline, wandering attention and anger are on the increase among girls as well. So, why is this culture having such a problem with passing on its values to the next generation?

Moralists say this failure to control our children results from the breakdown of traditional authority, which used to be rooted in the church, the school and the home. Their solutions are authoritarian and punitive. Some children are to be coerced to stay at school by tagging, others are to be brutally excluded.

Firm lines are to be drawn between the decent and the wicked. Theirs is a model of authority based on the old father-dominated family where disobedience would be severely punished. Jack Straw's discourse is not so different.

Hankering for authority is to be expected from right-wing traditionalists, but it is more surprising to find those who vigorously oppose the punitive mentality also expressing concern at a lack of parental authority. The word 'authority' also features among those who believe that the disruptive child is not a devil but is often a disturbed and distressed, vulnerable child. In the last few years in America, such children have been turned around by programmes which use a combination of consistent attention, behaviourist techniques and, crucially, restoring the parents' confidence in controlling their children; these programmes are currently being adopted in a number of American states to deal with that most difficult group, adolescents in care. Early intervention through these programmes convinced the UK Audit Commission in 1997 that they are more cost-effective than authoritarian punishment.

There are now a number of individuals and units who have adopted these models in the UK. In 1997, film-maker Roger Graef made *Breaking the Cycle* which followed the work of one such unit, the Marlborough House Day Unit, in its attempt to address and turn round the disruptive behaviour of children. The film shows how the unit deals with a group of pre-school children whose disruptive, anti-social and aggressive behaviour looks like the beginnings of a classic conflict with authority likely to end with their exclusion from school. In this film, we see the children change, not through the imposition of the sharp shock of traditional authoritarianism but because the parents learn different ways of handling their children's difficult moments.

The film shows that these children have become locked into patterns of behaviour which are constantly perceived as naughty. They see themselves as bad, have not developed the capacity to concentrate and are constantly in situations where no one can control them. In the Marlborough House Day Unit

183

the children are made to complete tasks and activities; bad behaviour is ignored; gentle restraint is often used; and the children are always praised. By the end of a ten-week course, most of the children are able to hear praise, concentrate, and actively share in the group ethos.

The theory behind this is that anti-social children are frightened because they feel out of control and no one will control them. This leads to aggression and a constant testing of the limits. So the central terms in countering this challenging behaviour are consistency, firmness, the building of self-esteem and, most importantly, encouraging the parents gently to resume control. There is no suggestion that the parents shown in this programme are any different from most families across the country. Many who watched the film recognized a familiar spiral: trying to negotiate gently with a child, who pushes the limits and provokes the parents into inconsistent attempts at control; the situation sometimes escalates into violence.

Loss of parental authority is a key part of the problem. 'There have been changes in how families are conducting their business,' says Peter Wilson. 'There used to be greater predictability, greater clarity about where you stood in relation to others, authority was more rigidly defined.' He adds: 'And children do need that. They look for consistency, reliability, clarity. You can only get that when you know where authority is' (interview with author). The changes in the family are symptoms of a period of profound change. In particular there is uncertainty about the roles of men and women in the family. The old authoritarianism of the father has died, and with it the structures which mirrored it: the patriarchal church and the authoritarian school. While the 'moralistic response' mourns the passing of the patriarchal order, the majority, whatever their party political views, are probably not sorry to see it go. The power of the patriarch was unearned. It often abused human rights, was violent and dictatorial, and terrifying for those in its power. And if the pay-off was relatively controllable children, the price was almost certainly the gross subordination of women.

At the same time, the power vacuum in the contemporary family has left women in an uncomfortable position. With women demanding more status and both men and women reluctant to allow men their old authority, women have been left on the front line of building a moral and disciplinary order in their families. Deprived of the authoritarian father, and the support of external institutions built on its model, families now have to make the rules up as they go along. This is no collapse of a moral order but the difficult birth of a new morality that tries to avoid the old authoritarianism and instil morality without fear. We are living in a society which believes that parents should never smack their children but mourns the lack of firm discipline.

Evolving a liberal morality requires both good structures of outside support and strong, confident people who can invent the rules, stick to them consistently, and do so without becoming violent and authoritarian. One of the problems here is that women's self-esteem has not necessarily matched the structural changes. Most women are not that confident in their authority, nor are there many places, such as the old extended family or the community of mothers, to turn to for relief and back-up. It is hard not to feel bitterly disappointed in self and child when what started as an attempt to be a child's friend spirals towards endless negativity. Obviously these problems are much greater for families under the stress of low pay, unemployment, and poor quality of life. Then it can become quite simply impossible to deal with children who have not been subdued by other external forms of authority. And this is not helped by the insistence of some feminists that women can manage all this perfectly well on their own.

Undoubtedly, this great collective effort to remake the basics of parenting is what has turned our schools into such a moral battleground. They are currently the last surviving places of community in our society, so they seem to embody the collective ability to parent. What has fallen heavily on schools is an expectation that they will control the children in their care, making them accept authority. In the past a number of external agencies would have backed up parental authority, especially if it was tottering; now there is only school and this is a heavy burden placed upon it.

All of which is to say that there are far more issues at stake in the anxiety about boys than may superficially appear. Some come from the pathologizing of masculinity, some come from anxieties about the social changes in the wake of disruptions to old class and race divisions, and some from a general crisis around parenting and the transmission of values in a non-patriarchal culture. It's only when we have teased out these elements in the equation that any sense can be made of whether there really is a specific problem about boys. What emerges is a very different picture. Instead of the amoral terrifying boy, boys are revealed as being at the sharp end of social changes and in very great danger of being blamed for all the discomforts which our society is experiencing in the process of that change. They are bearing the brunt – at least in public rhetoric – of the lack of clarity about what society wants men to be.

The previous chapters have exposed the inadequacies of the old assumptions about male power and female vulnerability. A much more muddled picture has emerged, in which men are sometimes vulnerable and women can have great authority, although often without the means to deal with this. The old debates about which sex has power, and which is oppressed, are hardly relevant in our transformed landscape once the complexities of men's and women's relationships are acknowledged. This is not just in the arenas of families, parenting, or representations of masculinity and boys; it is especially critical when these terms come to limit how sexuality can be expressed.

Sexual harassment is one such issue. In the clearer days of 1970s feminism, sexual harassment seemed self-evidently the way in which male economic potency was played out in social and emotional behaviour. In this new landscape most individuals feel that questions of sexual initiation and response are very confused. Even so, few of these doubts have yet found a voice. When it comes to looking at the question of sexual relations and how they are actually lived, we are dragged back into gender simplicities; the only terms available are 'rights', 'power', 'oppressors' and 'victims' and these are pinned consistently on one sex or the other. In popular culture, however, gender confusions are more visible.

American author Michael Crichton, when looking for a hair-raising plot to equal the impact of his novel *Jurassic Park*, asked himself what could be more terrifying than Tyrannosaurus Rex. In answer he hit on the supposedly terrifying scenario of a man being sexually harassed by his female boss. His book, *Disclosure*, was an instant success and almost immediately went into production as a film starring Demi Moore and Michael Douglas. His instinct for what might be terrifying to the 1990s subconscious was sound. Given the widespread perception of women in the ascendency over increasingly impotent men, it was hardly surprising that the image of the potent woman in the late 1980s began to assume somewhat terrifying proportions.

The omens were good for a film about a predatory female. The reception of *Fatal Attraction* was already history when *Disclosure* was written. Men stood up and clapped when the obsessive, menacing, predatory female played by Glenn Close finally got her comeuppance. Yet for all the feminist outrage at *Fatal Attraction*, this film had not explicitly set itself up as a crusade against feminist interpretations of sexual relations. In fact, the ending was remade several times until the producers finally found the one that appealed to the audiences. *Fatal Attraction* was as much part of a Hollywood tradition of the sexually powerful and frightening woman as it was a critical portrayal of contemporary career women. Its lineage was *Whatever Happened to Baby Jane?* and *Who's Afraid of Virginia Woolf?* rather than the ascent of woman. What belonged specifically to the late 1980s, however, was the appearance of the male victim, visibly less potent than the glamorous career woman, a man whose heroism came from transcending victim status to protect his family.

Disclosure, however, was different. This was no longer accidentally offending feminists by portraying an unmarried career woman as a potentially murderous obsessive. The terrain had shifted and feminism was now being addressed head on, in a reaction against the distortion of 'normal' sexual intercourse by positive discrimination and anti-harassment programmes. In *Disclosure*, Meredith Johnson is presented as a powerful woman who abuses her superior position to demand sex from her former lover (played by Michael Douglas). When he eventually refuses, after having been aroused, she claims that she has been harassed by him.

Disclosure was a milestone film, just as David Mamet's *Oleanna* had been a milestone play. *Oleanna* is the story of a university lecturer who is accused, in ambiguous circumstances, of sexual harassment by a female student. The drama centres on her manipulation of feminist-inspired legislation for personal ends. Both *Disclosure* and *Oleanna* bore witness to a growing reaction in American popular culture against the perceived advantages given to women by feminist discourse in general and anti-harassment legislation in particular. *Oleanna* was asking whether or not the concept of sexual harassment was being used by women in inappropriate circumstances. *Disclosure* was asking whether, with women now reaching higher positions in jobs, sometimes even in positions of power over men, it was not possible that they too could exploit that power for sexual favours. If women can have real power and authority, is it not possible they will exploit that power in the same way men have done?

Beyond those thoughts, of course, lies a more radical one. Is it possible that models of power and victimization might be used to muddy difficulties which both sexes are experiencing around sexual initiation and rejection? Katie Roiphe pursued this thought in her book *The Morning After*, much to the indignation of more traditional feminists, but her exposé of some of the sexual harassment propaganda is not so preposterous. In some American universities attempts to produce codes for appropriate sexual conduct and how to spot sexual harassment had become absurd. It is ridiculous to try and legislate for 'appropriate' forms of sexual advances and even more ridiculous to make subjective feelings of 'individual discomfort' the basis for recognizing the difference between harassment and welcome attention since that draws much too firm a line between getting it a bit wrong and being seen as a criminal predator.

Neither the novel nor the film of *Disclosure* dismisses sexual harassment legislation as totally unnecessary, but they do make radical points about this legislation. Marketed as a tale of our times, the main focus of *Disclosure* is on the abuse of power in work. Michael Crichton's claim is that if the feminist proposition is true, namely that sexual harassment is about power and not sex, then surely powerful women must be capable of doing it to less powerful men? His thesis is that as the number of women in power increases so does the number of women harassing men. Sexual harassment therefore is a men's issue too.

There are many feminists who find this completely unacceptable. Men, they say, can never be touched, coerced into sex or surrounded by intimidating sexual comments and innuendo in the way that women can be, and these are the actions that led to the original formulation of sexual harassment legislation. They argue that since society is male-dominated, occasional reversals of power in the work situation would not suddenly invert the dynamic of sexuality outside in society. But growing numbers of sexual harassment cases are brought by men, and the Industrial Society's book, *Sex at Work* (1998), 'accepts that men can be sexually harassed as well as women'.

My own more haphazard enquiries also indicate that while there are not overwhelming numbers of such cases, they are not unheard of. One woman I interviewed for an article on this subject was a film producer in her mid-forties. She has scores of credits to her name, but one she'd rather forget about. Several years ago she employed a young male director to work for her. She became besotted with him, and when he started an affair with a young actress she set out to hurt him.

> I don't understand why I became obsessed with him. He was pretty sexist, flirting all the time with women, but I tried very hard to make him respond to me, engineering all sorts of extra intimate meetings. When he started flaunting this affair with a younger woman, I was beside myself. He was married at the time so I sent an anonymous note to his wife. I started criticizing everything he did and trying my utmost to turn everyone against him.
>
> It wasn't difficult. The office was all female and it was easy to whip up disapproval about his extra-marital affair. They didn't cooperate with him and he started making mistakes. Eventually my partner decided to sack him. In retrospect, I

do think I used my position to harm him, although I think he behaved badly too. He flaunted his affair to hurt me. I don't know why.

This admission hardly makes her more frightening than Tyrannosaurus Rex on the warpath, but it is a clear indication that women can also, in a way that is only human, mix up sexual and working relationships. And if women are in power over men, they can use that position either to persuade a man into sex or to take revenge for a perceived slight.

This incident is, however, quite tame in the scale of things, certainly more tame than many of the cases brought against men for sexual harassment. A woman barrister, specializing in employment law, told me she was unable to confirm that sexual harassment of men is as common as the media seem to think. The problem is still far more likely to affect women. And the cases which women are involved in are often extreme, involving flagrant and specific sexual advances, threats of the consequences of non-compliance, and sexual humiliation by jokes and remarks. In predominantly male areas of work, this is not actually uncommon; there have been several high-profile cases recently in Britain which have exposed that in some police forces and fire services, sexual innuendo and harassment are still used to undermine women's confidence. However, she acknowledges that the sexual harassment of men does happen:

> Recently I dealt with an Indian doctor at a major teaching hospital who was in terrible distress because he was being pursued by a nurse. She phoned him at all hours and, when he had to sleep at the hospital, she even came into his bedroom. It was a case of physical and mental abuse but when he told the consultant he said, 'I should be so lucky'. (Interview with author)

Nor is it particularly difficult to find men who at least believe they have been harassed by women. Barry, who went to work in a London stockbroking firm at the age of twenty-five, was tormented by his boss, the woman office manager who was in her early thirties:

> At first we got along pretty well. I found her attractive, but because we were working together I thought it was better to keep at arm's length. We saw each other socially a bit, but I was never really aware of anything starting to happen sexually. One evening we went out for dinner. We went back to her flat and were chatting on the sofa when she leant over and kissed me. I confess I thought, 'Great!' She was older than me, more mature and she was keen on me. It was flattering. So one thing led to another. (Interview with author)

After a fortnight, he began to have 'serious doubts'. He had a girlfriend in Bristol and began to think he wanted to be with her again. He was also anxious about the complications of having a sexual relationship with a colleague and not so 'in love' that he was prepared to risk those complications:

> I arranged to see my boss and said we should finish it. Her attitude changed immediately. She set about trying to make my life hell. She abused me continuously and humiliated me in front of other colleagues. At meetings she would ask me why I had failed to do something (which I knew nothing about) and make out I was completely incompetent. She slagged me off to the partners.
>
> But while she was doing this she also made up to me. I never knew whether I was going to get vitriolic abuse or sweetness and light. On one occasion after she had given me several days of rotten abuse, she came up to me when I was at the coffee machine, put her arm around me, pressed herself up against me and asked if I had thought any more about our relationship. It was ghastly. I was on the point of blowing the gaff and then the partners would have to choose between us. But they had already sussed what was going on and they moved me from administration to become a trainee stockbroker.

Ironically, Barry thinks the whole episode may have helped his career. It moved him earlier than was usual out of administration. 'It was also', he says, 'a hell of a good lesson. It's the best cure I can think of for adultery.' To many this may sound like the messy consequences of an ill-judged relationship rather than harassment. However, the employment barrister disagrees: 'This situation fits the legal definition of sexual harassment. This woman was sexually tormenting this man and using her power over him to do so. Sexual harassment also includes making the working environment hostile by using sexuality and sexual references to degrade and upset the recipients. It fits on this count too.'

It is this phenomenon – the powerful but scorned woman – that has led the media to construct the image of a sexually rapacious, power-mad female. Women may not be able to rape but they sure can take revenge. And Meredith Johnson, the protagonist of *Disclosure*, is a real 'bunny boiler', as such women have come to be known after the scene in *Fatal Attraction* when Glenn Close as the jilted lover cooks the family rabbit. She is a stereotype of single-minded careerist with a voracious sexual appetite, a desire to dominate men, no domestic life and no conscience.

In an age when women still hold far fewer positions of power than men and where it is not exactly commonplace for them to take (and maintain) the sexual initiative, this stereotype seems misogynistic. However, Barry's experience suggests there might be a grain of truth in male fears. He thinks he suffered not because women are predatory monsters but because women are not good at handling rejection. There is something potentially lethal in the combination of women with power but without sufficient experience in how to take the sexual initiative and deal with rejection. Barry says:

Men have more training in sexual rejection. If you've been trying since the age of thirteen to get girls to go out with you, you get used to a high failure rate in sex. At an early age in an affair, there's a lot of testing the water. You go out to dinner, or the theatre or even to bed. But when it comes to the crunch a woman might say, 'You're nice, but I don't find you sexually attractive.' Usually you just accept that. It's not the end of the world.

It's certainly the case that in spite of decades of feminism arguing that girls should feel able to take as much initiative as men, and in spite of new media stereotypes of the sexually assertive woman, girls and boys are still growing up with remarkably stereotyped notions of who should and should not make the running in sexual relationships. Girls who take the initiative or represent themselves as enjoying and actively seeking out sexual encounters are still likely at some point to be stigmatized, and sometimes with serious consequences. In 1993, Matthew Kydd was cleared of rape on a date rape charge, his main defence having been conducted in terms of the accuser's sexual rapaciousness; she was described as having been sexually promiscuous and having won the student award of slag of the year.

Sexual rejection obviously plays a part in some forms of men's sexual harassment of women; women who have rejected their bosses' sexual advances have often been 'punished' for it. In pre-feminist days, some university careers flourished or faded according to the status of the professor's sexual interest (which made the misunderstood professor of *Oleanna* seem so preposterous to some women). Barry's experience, however, suggests that women's inexperience with rejection can create its own problems. Rejection can be more difficult for a woman, especially if she has made the first move. We shouldn't imagine that just because she *is* a woman, she would be beyond using a position of power to settle old scores.

What a few individuals might hypothetically do in the heat of an unrequited passion, however, hardly amounts to a major trend as the media like to suggest. It is important to get a clear perspective on the issue, the truth of which may be different from the two hard-line versions which have been dominating understanding of this topic. In the hard-line feminist view, no woman can ever sexually harass a man because men have power, full stop. That power will reassert itself in any sexual exchange even if the woman has more power at work than the man in question. In this version, women can never sexually harass because they do not have the back-up of the threat of real physical violence or force which they say lies behind men's harassment of women. But the hard-line anti-feminist view is just as ridiculous, not to say paranoid: all sexual harassment claims against men are seen as distortions of the truth. In this version, all claims of sexual harassment come about either because of power-mad female harassers or from harridans wielding the weapons of political correctness in their vendettas against men.

For many in the UK, neither of these stereotypes seems very useful, dogged as they are by the desire to establish which sex has power. In the UK it is hardly the case that employers cannot move because they are so hemmed in by draconian anti-male legislation. There are still many employers who have not even considered the issue of proper policies against harassment. These are much less frequent between boss and employee than in situations where one sex is in dominance over another. Occupational health workers tell the real situation of harassment of women. They describe time lost by women workers through depression and fear. They quote cases like that of Mrs Sheila Wagstaff, who won the maximum £8,925 compensation at a Leeds industrial tribunal in 1991 after years of torment in an electronics store, which included a colleague shoving his penis in her ear. They will also tell you of their hopes that Britain will eventually take up European Union recommendations that all companies should have a policy or face liability in such cases.

Similarly, the reality of the harassment of men in Britain tends to be different from the image portrayed by the media. This is much more likely to occur in all-female environments or where a women's culture predominates, such as in a super-market or factory. Sheila Brewer, senior labour relations officer at the Royal College of Nursing, says: 'It's easy to imagine in a predominantly female culture like nursing that the women can gang up on a young man. An older, experienced female nurse

195

might make a young man do all sorts of horrendous jobs' (interview with author). One of the few cases in Britain where the man's complaint was upheld was in 1996 when a junior doctor complained he had been 'victimized by a ward full of women'.

The reality of sexual harassment is very different from the media image, though there is one important aspect that *Disclosure* did get right and which we would be foolish to overlook. There *is* a very real issue for men around disclosure, both for men who are being taunted and for those manipulated by a female superior. Simon Biggs, a psychologist who has worked in social services, says: 'There are a number of norms at play which make it very difficult for men to make disclosures. Men are expected to want sex. Women are expected to resist' (interview with author). Biggs thinks this is because it is not easy for a man to say he has been manipulated into a sexual situation he doesn't really want to be in: 'If he tells other men, he's not likely to get much sympathy. They might say, "Lucky old you", or, "At least you're getting it", or, "Just tell her to get lost". He will find it hard to reveal he's been manipulated or finds it a negative experience.'

To make a disclosure about sexual harassment inevitably involves a man exposing his vulnerability. He has either been the butt of female hostility or he has allowed himself to be manipulated in some way. And our culture is very resistant to seeing men in these traditionally 'feminine' ways. Harassment of a man by a woman often consists of a subtle, emasculating process rather than direct physical threats. A woman cannot rape a man but she can manipulate him physically and if he has an orgasm there inevitably appears to be an element of consent.

Having stirred up the issue of the harassment of men, no one seems interested in thinking about it in these terms. For what lies at the heart of the issue is not just the capacity of both sexes to abuse power (as emphasized by Crichton), but the capacity of both sexes to be vulnerable. The media do not like to admit that male sexuality is not always predatory and in control, and that it can be responsive to women. But feminists who hang on to the idea that only men harass and only women can be harassed are equally wedded to the idea of male invulnerability. It's the same disregard of male vulnerability which has meant that many boys who have been sexually abused have been disregarded or given inadequate support.

Confronted with this unsettling possibility, both camps tend to prefer an easy solution. Anti-feminists have manufactured the image of the monstrous harpy sinking her claws into men. This mythical creation tells us nothing about real workplace experiences. Feminists insist this is a media fabrication but they too are closed to the possibility of male vulnerability. Both responses tell us much about our culture and our sexual expectations. Its not just men who are more comfortable with the idea of the phallic woman than with a 'feminine' and vulnerable man; it is women too.

If men can be vulnerable oppressors, then women can certainly be potent victims. When the issue of date rape arrived in Britain, as American trends inevitably do, these issues of sexual vulnerability and power were again at stake. They showed again how deeply entrenched are society's notions of male sexuality as powerful, initiatory and ultimately responsible for the outcome of sexual encounters.

A string of date rape cases, each with a different outcome, exposed just how confused attitudes towards sexuality and sexual responsibility have become in this post-feminist age. In Britain, three cases highlighted the problem; that of Angus Diggle charged and found guilty of raping his escort to a ball; Matthew Kydd, cleared of rape after he went on to have full sex with a girl with whom he had just had oral sex; and Austen Donnellan, cleared of charges that he raped a fellow student after they had ended up in bed together after a drunken party. Each one centred on questions of how appropriate it was in these circumstances to bring a rape charge.

Date rape is not new. In spite of myths persisting to the contrary, the majority of rapes are committed by men known to the victim. In 1992, for instance, a Home Office survey revealed that in only 30 per cent of rapes reported to the police was the attacker a stranger. In 35 per cent of the cases, he was an acquaintance, and in the rest an intimate (Sue Lees, *Carnal Knowledge*). Nevertheless, it is only recently that complaints like those mentioned above would have reached court.

In the days before sexual liberation, women who went 'so far' would not have assumed the right to be protected if they wanted to go 'no further'. Now, there is a growing acceptance, influenced by feminism, by the police, prosecutions and the courts, that women have a right to say no and to be listened to, whatever the circumstances.

Twenty or thirty years ago, the prosecution had to show that the man had induced a woman's submission by force, fear or fraud. As recently as 1982 Judge David Wild summed up a case with the comment:

> Women who say no do not always mean no. It's not just a question of saying no, it is a question of how she says it, how she shows and makes it clear. If she doesn't want it she only has to keep her legs shut and she would not get it without force and there will be marks of force having been used.

Officially, however, since the Sexual Offences Act in 1976, it has only to be proved that the man knew that the woman did not consent. Feminism has played an important role in changing these attitudes towards rape, challenging the sexist assumption that if a woman says no she may actually mean yes – an assumption about the probing initiatory nature of male sexuality and the passive nature of female sexuality.

Yet each of the high-profile cases which hit the British press in 1993, conveniently coinciding with Katie Roiphe's book on the subject, raised questions about whether or not women were now applying double standards to their sexual encounters. On the one hand they were laying claim to an unparalleled degree of freedom, both in terms of sexual behaviour and dress (sexual codes and conduct); on the other hand they were backing off from, and criminalizing, full penetrative sex in highly ambiguous circumstances.

Angus Diggle's case was perhaps less ambiguous than the subsequent ones. He had taken Miss X to a St Andrew's Night ball at the Grosvenor House Hotel. They both drank a lot and then spent the night in the house of a friend. She went to sleep on the couch, waking to find 'Diggle on top of her, holding her down and naked apart from his spectacles, the frilly cuffs of his highland dress and a green condom.' When police came to arrest him later, he is supposed to have said: 'Well, I've been out with her. I have spent £200 on her. Why can't I do what I did to her?' Diggle's defence was conducted in terms of his having thought that the woman had invited him to have sex; some time was spent during the trial trying to establish that the accuser was drunk and that her behaviour suggested a form of consent, but that didn't cut much ice.

Diggle did not command much sympathy; there were jokes about his name and revelations about his tastes and previous convictions for sexual harassment. This led to several articles in which he was depicted as a 'pathetic' figure, living alone with his mother, unable to get a job in the profession which he had trained. He provided an easy target to establish that, even on a date, no meant no, that consent to go out with a man did not mean consent to sex, and that women have every right to legal protection against rape.

Yet a slew of subsequent, far more ambiguous cases, instantly problematized the boundaries. The case which attracted most attention was that of Austen Donnellan, a student at King's College, London, who, controversially, went to the police himself. He had been accused of rape by a fellow student and friend and the college proposed to deal with the matter privately at a disciplinary committee. Donnellan was backed up by Lord Russell, his history tutor, and had always protested his innocence, refusing to be dealt with in this way. He was concerned that a college hearing would end in warnings and dismissal which could ruin his reputation and possibly his whole career. Since he insisted on his innocence, he preferred to take his chance at law.

Donnellan was accused of rape in circumstances more ambiguous than those surrounding Angus Diggle. He had been to a party with a friend and met up with the girl who later accused him of rape. He was alleged to have had a long-standing, largely unreciprocated sexual interest in her. On this occasion, at a pre-Christmas party, after a large amount of drink they ended up kissing and going back to her room. They were both so drunk that they fell over several times on the way there. He claimed he had sex with her consent; she claimed that she was raped. Her defence was that she was so drunk she could neither have given consent nor withheld it. It must have been rape because he must have known that she would never want full sex with him when sober as she found him 'physically repellent'.

Donnellan was eventually acquitted after the girl's case fell apart. She could not remember the details, therefore the judge suggested she could not possibly remember whether she did or did not withhold consent. But a huge storm of publicity followed, raising the question as to whether British students were now treading the path of American political correctness, trying to formulate very precise rules and regulations about sexual conduct between men and women in order to protect women from what the Americans called, a 'non-consensual contact of a sexual nature'.

Many commentators were appalled that this had ever come to court. They pointed out that in the days preceding 'political correctness' this would simply have been put down to 'bad sex'. As Louise Chunn, then editor of the *Guardian* women's page, put it, plenty of women in the post-liberation days have similar stories to tell:

> but with a different ending. They too have woken up in the morning after a drunken debauch, or sex 'for old times' sake' with an ex-lover, or next to a friend who lost his doorkey and was offered a bed for the night 'but nothing more' (I could go on and on ...) But they didn't call their lawyers, they marked it down to experience. (*Guardian*, 20 October 1993)

Linda Grant in *The War of the Words* (1994) recounted her version in similarly amusing vein:

> What did the woman do next? By the end of the afternoon she'd pretty well forgotten about the night before. She did not feel defiled. She did not shower a dozen times, scrubbing

at her skin. She did not feel her identity evaporate. She did not call the police. She did not inform the university authorities. She did not confront the man. What she did was to tell a number of people what had happened and it was agreed it was typical of him – he was an egocentric arrogant bastard; that was the consensus. Everyone felt sorry for his girlfriend but no one told her. No one suggested the woman should go for counselling. No one held her. She didn't develop an eating disorder and she was never able afterwards to feel the event was a trauma. She just had it down as a bad night.

It is possible to imagine that bad sex in the wrong circumstances is rape only if you adhere to a model of male power where heterosexual penetration is an expression of that power and is therefore a crime against a less powerful group rather than a probable outcome in an explicit sexual encounter between a man and a woman. It works only if you assume women are not fully responsible for their sexuality. If, on the contrary, you assume women are sexual equals, then it is a double standard to assume that male sexual pushiness expresses male power while female sexual forwardness does not. It is a double standard, too, to think it is OK for women to have sexual feelings and go a certain distance, but not OK for men to go their distance because penetrative sex is an expression of power. The assumption is that women's sexuality can never hurt whereas penetration is always an act of violence; clear echoes here of the radical feminist Andrea Dworkin who once said: 'The hurting of women . . . is basic to the pleasure of man' (quoted in *Sunday Times*, 24 October 1993).

What was also exposed by the Donnellan case was the question of responsibility. Making a charge of rape under such circumstances suggested that the girl felt that the ultimate responsibility for the sex act lay with the man. Her drunkenness was put forward as an explanation for how she came to be in the situation; his drunkenness, however, could not excuse what he did. Again there were echoes of American campus feminism.

Mary Koss, Professor of Psychology at Arizona University and author of *The Scope of Rape* (1993), claims that in 70 per cent of all date rape cases excessive use of alcohol is involved. Her conclusion is not that both sexes have equal responsibility in such circumstances but that men have special responsibilities. In bizarre language she claims: 'The law punishes the drunk driver who kills a pedestrian. Likewise the law needs to be here to protect the drunk woman from the driver of the penis' (quoted in *Sunday Times*, 24 October 1993).

In less ambiguous circumstances this thinking might be comprehensible. In any sexual encounter there should be a let-out clause for both sexes. There may well come a point when either the man or the woman might not want to go on. And while it is difficult for a woman to force it, it is not so difficult for a man. In circumstances where both sexes have already gone a certain distance and where both are almost incapably drunk, it is not impossible to imagine that a man too might go through with something he does not necessarily want or think is a particularly good idea. The question is whether in such situations we can really equate unwanted penetration with rape – penetration against our will.

There is a dangerous logic attached to opening up such questions. In the case of Matthew Kydd, which followed close on the heels of that of Austen Donnellan, many of the old-fashioned stereotypes which had deprived women of protection in the past were again mobilized. The circumstances were in many ways similar. There was a drunken party. Kydd had been invited back to her room. Both were drunk, both had stripped off and had consensual oral sex; he had gone on to have full penetrative sex. She reported it two days later when, on reflection, she decided it had been rape. This time the defence was conducted in terms of the girl's previous character. The papers gleefully repeated defence lawyers' claims that she had won the title 'slag of the year', that she was known for sexually promiscuous behaviour and had played strip poker with two men who refused sex with her because she 'smelt horrible'. As the girl rather plaintively said herself, she didn't see what her other behaviour had to do with it and surely someone was entitled to change their mind.

Most of the attention paid to these cases focused on the question of anonymity: why should the principle of anonymity not be extended to both accuser and accused? Interestingly, Donnellan himself wrote several articles warning against any attempts to solve this anomaly by removing anonymity for rape victims. In one article he explained that he thought the principle of anonymity had been hard won by women; guarantees of anonymity had been crucial in helping women come forward in rape cases. What bothered Donnellan was that the exposure of his case in the papers meant that he would always have to live in the shadow of these accusations. The issue of anonymity, though, was something of a side-track. What was really at issue was the double standard. Are women really entitled to be as liberated as they want to be, but men not? Are women able to be as explicit in their expression of sexuality up to and even including orgasm, and not accepting that a man acting in an equivalent way might assume this would involve the orgasm of penetrative sex? Is it the case that in a supposedly egalitarian context, where equal treatment and rights are demanded at all other levels, the act of penetration is really the wielding of some instrument of cruelty?

To ask such questions is not to deny the seriousness of rape or that women should be protected not just from violence but also from the unwelcome imposition of sex. Nor that, in these days of Aids, that men and women should be able to give and receive sexual pleasure without necessarily having penetrative sex. But isn't there also a question of responsibility here too? Is it really only up to the men to 'control' themselves?

One of the consequences of feminism's insistence that women's sexual self-expression is an act of defiance against patriarchal domination is that support has been given to all sorts of dubious logic surrounding this question. Daisy Waugh, sticking up for the female student involved in the Austen Donnellan case, is quoted as saying: 'however much a woman has been drinking, however provocative she is, it is the man's responsibility to control himself. If he can't trust himself at any point, he should not spend time alone with a woman. Women are entitled to be as liberated as they like' (*Daily Mail*, 20 October 1993). This is a view of female sexuality which has spread much further than feminism. We hear it from the mouths of actresses like Sharon Stone, defending the notorious shot of her genitals in *Basic Instinct*; from supermodels consenting to pose in clothes like those of Versace which appear to display women's bodies in degrading ways; and from porn stars and Page 3 girls. If they adopt poses denoting they are sexually aroused and ready for sex, this does not mean that they are, well, ready for sex. Instead, they are celebrating their sexuality, enjoying the power which derives from having a desirable body. In Britain, recent debates over the proliferation of men's magazines which share so much of the visual rhetoric of porn magazines brought forth many of these clichés. Zoe Ball was quoted as saying posing is all harmless fun, while Emma Wright, hostess of television's *The Price is Right*, can think of nothing that has given her 'more of an ego-boost' than featuring on the pages of one such magazine, *Maxim*. Such images, she claims, give a strong and positive message for women in the 1990s: 'these are women celebrating their sexuality. They are proud, confident and in charge.' Joanna Guest, a topless model, adds: 'Men may drool over pictures of me naked. But I know what I am doing and the effect I can have. And that's very empowering.' (All quoted in *Daily Mirror*, 29 August 1997.)

These are the familiar '90s show-biz clichés; it is claimed women are now in control of their sexuality; they dress (or undress) for themselves, not men. When they flaunt their sexuality it is flaunting a power previously denied to women. Madonna made such views fashionable and the Spice Girls have made them ordinary. It is not surprising that minor celebrities and models grab these lines. They move in a world where flaunting it is *de rigueur* so long as, well, the price is right. In the past a woman who sold images of her body for money did so in the seedy world of prostitution and pornography. Now, ironically, she can bolster herself with fragments of feminist discourse. If men are assumed to be sexual oppressors, then there is status to be had from demonstrating an available sexuality which is powerful enough to lure men but at the same time to resist them.

According to Natasha Walker author of *The New Feminism*:

> It's fair enough that women should feel there's a kind of moral value in a woman standing up and saying, 'I'm going to express my sexuality' in a way that there isn't for a man because a man's always had that right. Young girls have traditionally felt themselves beholden to act modestly and quietly and you know all the advice I had in teen magazines when I was a young girl said 'when you're out on a date with a boy ask him about himself, don't talk too much about yourself. I think it has real moral value if that is cut through – if there's something like the Spice Girls and other girl bands around saying 'we're not going to behave like that'. I don't think it's hypocritical. I think it's good. (Interview with author).

We are all supposed to be in awe of how these women in the public eye appear to have a new attitude towards sexuality, but their feminist rhetoric is a con. All it shows is that they have little regard for the situation of women outside their own protected milieu. It is all very well for powerful women in the media to assert new clichés about female sexual potency, but harder for the wannabes and lookalikes to live these on the streets. For the majority of women move in a world where it is not so easy to draw a line between provoking men to drool and getting something more unwelcome. This is, after all, a society in which women do not have the same freedom of movement as men, and where rape or sexual attack are more than remote theoretical possibilities. In this world, if men talked about 'celebrating' their sexuality or the power they felt from putting it about, we would probably want to lock them up.

Away from the fantasies contained in public images, issues such as attracting, asserting and taking the initiative cause confusion, as the date rape cases show; and it is not just girls who are in difficulty here. 'The big change for adolescent men in the last ten years', says Dr Fieldman from St George's Medical School, 'is the conflicting and imprecise codes they receive from adolescent girls.' Elaborating on this, Paul Farmer of the Samaritans says that, in the past,

> young men were predatory, girls were willing but selective prey. If a young man was rebuffed his ego was bruised but it was in the context of a mutually understood set of rules. Now some males perceive that feminism and political correctness have made women the opposing team and the referee. They perceive the risks of getting it wrong to be far greater than mere rejection. (Quoted in *Observer*, 31 October 1993)

We are being encouraged to think that it is acceptable for a girl to assert her sexuality by behaving provocatively and unacceptable for a man to respond as if that was an invitation. This confusion seems to be growing. On the one hand, rape cases are still bedeviled by the inappropriate questioning of victims, as Sue Lees' book *Carnal Knowledge* (1996) makes clear. In it she shows that in rape cases the victim is still interrogated as to how much she may have led the man on, an inappropriate and destructive line of questioning given that the psychology of rape often has nothing to do with the behaviour of the victim.

On the other hand, other cases indicate that some women may be turning to the law to draw the boundaries which they have failed to draw in their own sexual behaviour. These are not abstract cases with little effect on real lives. Helen Garner's book, *The First Stone* (1997), traces a harassment case brought against an Australian university lecturer by two young women. He was eventually acquitted because the behaviour and evidence of the girls who brought the case were extremely ambivalent. Garner was shocked to find that the woman who brought the case used feminism to justify what she saw as a double standard in sex. The unproven allegations ruined the university lecturer's reputation.

Such were the ambiguities of this particular case that, even after reading the book (in which Garner is very much in sympathy with the lecturer), I remained in doubt about what had actually happened. Had the lecturer talked dirty about a provocative picture he kept of one of the students on his desk and then assaulted her? Or had she behaved provocatively, gone along to his office where they both talked dirty and then fabricated an assault charge motivated by other grievances against him?

In fact, Garner's book is not really concerned with proving or disproving the allegations. What concerns her is the resort to law over a relatively minor sexual incident in which the girl's openly inviting sexual behaviour might be said to have played a part. What Garner wanted to challenge was the 'article of faith' which she observed among young feminists that they have a right to dress and behave as they please – explicit displays of sexual alertness which they would not allow to men:

> to dress to display your body and then to project all the sexuality of the situation onto men and blame them for it just so that you can continue to feel innocent and put upon is dishonest and irresponsible. Worse, it is relinquishing power. If a woman dresses to captivate, she'd better learn to keep her wits about her, for when the wrong fish swims into the net.

Needless to say, Garner met with a huge amount of hostility when her views became known, doubtless because she was attacking what has become another sacred cow of feminist thinking: that women's sexual self-expression is not an act of invitation but an act of political defiance. A recent case in England against a lecturer at Reading University uncannily echoed what happened in Australia and emphasized the curious feminist logic, insisting on equality in one breath while conjuring up vulnerability in another. John Cunningham was accused of indecent assault by two girls, and acquitted. The jury were apparently baffled by how he managed to assault both girls simultaneously without one of them managing to sound an alarm.

In this case, as in the Australian case, a double standard was at work. The girls were operating with a degree of sexual forwardness which was denied to the men involved. Such cases are arriving in court because of what has become a muddled truth of our age; men have real and dangerous power whereas women's assertive sexuality is only an act of bravado. When everyday situations no longer have clear boundaries, individuals turn to the law to establish boundaries for them. In all the cases discussed, including the acquittals, there have been real victims, but not just the women as feminism might have it. All the protagonists have been crucified by the legal process for the crime of taking female sexual forwardness literally rather than treating it with the ironic post-modern distance claimed for it by public figures.

When the boundaries between the sexes have none of the old clarity, legislation is not an effective way of redrawing them. Indeed, if the law is to have any use as a protection against sexual violence and sexual cruelty, then in the more ambiguous areas of sexual intimacies it should have no place. We are now in a world where even the President of the United States can be challenged by the possibility that he has exploited women, as happened when Paula Jones claimed to have been sexually harassed and therefore entitled to legal compensation. So we must also live in a world where women have enough power to take responsibility for their own actions.

CONCLUSION

This book begins with a question: Is feminism relevant to the new millennium? So the conclusion must involve an answer.

Feminism was a hugely important social doctrine. Both its aims and much of what it taught us remain relevant. But feminism has not fully faced up to the changes for which it was partly responsible. It often continues to peddle a version of gender relations in society which can have unfortunate consequences, especially when it merges with bigotry to attack vulnerable men. In that respect, it has become an outmoded ideology increasingly unable to make sense of a very different society.

I have discussed how important feminism has been both to myself and to society in general. There will be no going back on the things which feminism changed and I personally would not want there to be. Feminism bequeathed certain aims which will never become irrelevant; justice and equality between the sexes should always be important for any modern vibrant democracy. Some of the lessons that feminism taught are equally important. After feminism, there can be no going back to the idea of male domination built on a 'natural' order. Feminism taught us to pay attention to gender division, sex roles and sexual behaviour, and to realize that they might entail the workings of power. It made it impossible for us ever again to accept as givens those divisions of labour which are based on social discrimination. Still more, feminism changed what we value as a society, making the aims of sexual intimacy and equality, equal parenting, and non-hierarchical family relations part of the democratic ideals of any modern society. So, as a set of ideals which will always require vigilance, feminism remains as relevant as ever.

Feminism, though, is a victim of its own success. In many instances it has failed to notice how much society and men have changed in response to its demands. Instead, it has continued to insist that society is as sexually divided as ever, and with much the same effects. But as this book has shown, gender divisions no longer operate as they did in the days before feminism emerged. The picture is much more complex. Now we have an economy that is in many ways gender-blind, and it has developed in such a way that it has created tremendous upheavals, especially in men's expectations. Feminism set women on a path which made them acceptable, possibly even profiteers, in this new landscape. Yet many insist on their continued disadvantages. Men meanwhile have often found themselves not only disadvantaged but disparaged as potentates, even as their power base crumbled.

Feminists have kept up their hostility to male power on the grounds that, whatever economic and legal changes there are, men still retain moral authority. I have disputed this linchpin of feminist ideology as well. The combination of feminism and changes in the economy have shattered the easy way in which men could assume that their masculinity entitled them to a superior position. The uncertainty which men have been feeling and the effect of this on the socialization of boys show how inadequate it is to assume the all-importance of gender division, categorizing men into powerful positions and women into subordinate ones. It was the potential power of the father which gave men of all classes that possibility, and that has gone. Now we have to acknowledge that gender is only one among many divisions in a truly uneven and heterogeneous society.

Yet everyone keeps looking for an easy answer about the state of gender relations. Those who acknowledge that men do not have the same power they used to, tend to assume that now women have the power and men are the victims. Both Melanie Phillips and Fay Weldon talk about a new matriarchy, but this way of looking at it is part of the problem. It is stuck in an old model of sexual power, where one sex consistently has power across the board. In reality, no one sex has it in the way men did in a father-dominated society. The social upheavals, new divisions, and changing values of masculinity and femininity have seen to that. However abstract your terms of reference, it is impossible to find that consistent structural advantage which men had in pre-feminist days.

This is not to say that men do not often have a great deal of power over women. There are still many ways in which women are disadvantaged. Networking and men's narcissistic interest in each other often cut women out of positions of power. Sexual attitudes are often denigratory. Male hostility to women is still a significant social fact. Old sexual attitudes remain highly problematic, especially for vulnerable women; rape, sexual violence and harassment are all real not imaginary problems. Depending on who you are and where you are, being a woman can often still feel unfairly difficult.

There are other ways in which women are benefiting in the current society. They have the advantages of greater self-esteem, of better expectations and, if the truth were known, of more satisfying choices. There are also powerful women now, and women can be the breadwinners. Conversely, men can find themselves disadvantaged – finding it as difficult to break into female areas of work as women ever did to break into men's – and treated with sexual suspicion. Working-class men especially are the scapegoats of a society no longer at ease with masculinity.

So where does that leave the old feminist tenets? In the last few chapters I looked at contemporary social issues where discussion of gender is most pointed. What shows up there is just how difficult it is to cram what is going on back into the old sack of feminist 'truths'. It is no longer the case that one sex consistently oppresses the other or that one sex consistently occupies the position of oppressor or victim. The picture at the moment is much more muddled and uneven. Men are still often the beneficiaries of how gender works in this society, but now women sometimes are as well. It differs with different cases.

Even when masculinity is at its most oppressive, it may be

necessary to leave behind preconceptions of the male brute and accept a more complex picture where the construction of masculinity and femininity are inextricably interlinked. We may have to ask how much women have actively been involved in constructing the polarities of gender: how we position ourselves as women; what we ask of men; how we treat our sons; how we collude in creating men in the masculinity we claim to abhor. All these make a more confused picture in which women themselves are implicated. In short, this is not a society in which feminism's old descriptions work any longer. It doesn't have simple gender lines. It has many different occasions, practices, lifestyles and styles in which gender is a significant division but not one which consistently ascribes discrimination to one side of that division. Feminism's attitude towards this evolving society has been inconsistent. We've been hostile to men's attempts to change, operated with double standards and, most especially, continued to demand special pleading for women just as the whole of society is becoming so much more heterogeneous and complex.

After following the strands in all the different areas covered in this book – changing economic and social attitudes, the different meanings now attached to femininity and masculinity, the widespread sexual confusion – the pursuit of women's 'rights' in the old feminist terms begins to look problematic. Most feminists still fundamentally believe in continued vigilance around, perhaps even expansion of, women's rights. It is only through this route, they believe, that true and stable equality will be reached. Women's rights are seen as compensation for continued disadvantage and even when they appear to advantage women unfairly, we've managed to persuade most men to accept this. As Sean French put it: 'I'm in favour of the European court upholding the right to favour female applications . . . just as I was in favour of women-only short lists for Labour seats. But what would I have felt if it was me who was rejected in favour of one of these women? Bloody awful of course. Depressed. Unable to talk to anyone' (*Guardian*, 18 May 1998).

Yet it is precisely in the discourse around women's rights, and in the call for continued vigilance in this area, that the limitations of feminism as a politics rapidly become apparent. Everyone accepts in abstract that women's rights are a good thing, but looked at more closely they have been operating extremely unevenly in these changed times, sometimes even creating a major mess. This is different from saying that to promote women's rights is to deprive men. I'm saying something that is simultaneously much simpler, and requires more difficult solutions; that, before we know whose rights need defending, we need to know exactly where discrimination is occurring.

The working of equal opportunities legislation is a case in point. Throughout the 1990s, equal opportunities and sex discrimination legislation have disintegrated into chaos. Tribunals, set up to provide simple remedies, are becoming bogged down in arguments of the most arcane legal complexity. The legislation originally set up to level the playing field for women is now being used more often by men. Of course, not all cases brought by men have aimed to undermine the protection which sex discrimination legislation was supposed to give. Recent judgments on men's rights to free prescriptions and access to pensions contribute to greater sexual equality. Men also have a case about the profound discrimination which they experience in the caring professions. There is far more evidence of exclusion of men from traditional 'female' jobs now than of the exclusion of women from 'male' jobs.

Some cases *have* been able to use the Equal Opportunities Commission to make direct political challenges against instances of positive encouragement for women. The 'Equality Squad', a group of men, turned to the Equal Opportunities Commission to get help in challenging Leicester County Council for allowing the local library to hold women-only sessions for Muslim girls. This was not a one-off. Both the RAC's all-women safety classes and various all-women swimming clubs have been challenged through the legislation.

Most of the cases in the mid-1990s were more complex than

these. They showed growing evidence that deserving people were being put off the EOC's complex structures and some who needed protection were even getting hurt. For example, in February 1996, Police Sergeant Les White won a sex discrimination case. He had been accused by a woman police officer of making derogatory remarks and her complaint was upheld by the Metropolitan Police. He was fined and transferred to another police station. Later, he claimed the quality of his life had deteriorated. An industrial tribunal agreed that he had suffered from sex discrimination because he was transferred rather than his accuser, without having been given an equal opportunity to put his case. He won substantial damages. Thus the EOC compensated someone originally found guilty of undermining a female colleague.

Separate European legislation adds considerably to our own confusion. UK courts can refer to any of the many different forms of European law which set the legal framework around sex discrimination through directives, treaties, codes of practice or resolutions. The implications can be considerable. In 1996, a transsexual successfully used European directives on 'equal treatment'; the UK Sex Discrimination Act now appears to apply to all sexual minorities, although the law is currently so complex that even an EOC lawyer admits it is comprehensible only to lawyers. The EOC itself admits the need to simplify the situation under one new equal treatment law. But even if laws were simplified, the fundamental question remains: which groups, if any, need additional protection in our changing economy?

The feminist answer to this is clear: women. There are still more men in management, politics and industry and at higher levels; the famous glass ceiling still has to be broken through. And women still need support when they encounter discrimination in male cultures like the army, the police or the fire service. Mothers returning to work often face discrimination when they try to reduce hours or to job share. While this is indisputable, it does not necessarily amount to a situation where all women are more in need of support than men. The discrimination women still meet now takes place against a different backdrop. What is significant about the various attempts to challenge legislation set up to help women is that there is clearly no longer any consensus among the populace that women suffer from structural discrimination and need extra help.

One might wonder why feminists have not been in the forefront of challenging the ragbag of chaotic legislation with which the EOC is now operating in its name. One might want to ask, if discrimination legislation can be picked up successfully by both men and women, whether gender discrimination has now become something likely to affect both sexes at different times and is just one form of discrimination among a whole series of others that individuals might meet – which might include discrimination based on race, fat, looks or class. Nevertheless, calling for a rethink would be highly problematic. It would mean raising the question of whether discrimination against women is still systematic or just sporadic. It is clear that many women are deeply reluctant to let that idea go, along with its concomitant belief that because of this systematic discrimination women need extra help.

It is also for this reason that most feminists still have not dissociated themselves from the idea of positive discrimination. There has always been a thin line between creating opportunities and positive discrimination but, technically, positive discrimination is illegal in the UK. In the past, instances of positive encouragement for women would have gone unchallenged because everyone agreed that women were structurally disadvantaged. Now, legislation which was set up to equal things out for women is increasingly perceived as advantaging a minority where similar protection is not afforded to men.

In 1996 in the run-up to the British general election, the Labour Party initially supported all-women shortlists in order to guarantee more women Members of Parliament. When challenged as to the legality of this action, the leadership was quicker than its feminist supporters in recognizing that the tide had turned against anything that smacked of positive discrimination programmes. Ever attentive to events across the Atlantic, the Labour leadership knew that even in the USA, the heartland of positive discrimination programmes, such initiatives were being cut back and closed down. European precedent also warned against this course of action; in autumn 1995, Bremen City Council was told its positive discrimination employment practices contravened the European Union equal treatment directive.

The increase in the numbers of women shortlisted was justified not only on the grounds that it was unjust that so many more men became MPs than women; more women, it was believed, would make a significant difference to how politics was conducted and the sort of political objectives that would be pursued. Blair's victory in May 1997 seemed to justify some of the strategies. Psychologically, at the very least, there did seem something refreshing about the sea of women (over 100 MPs) who changed the very masculine appearance of the House of Commons. There was something very positive in knowing that women who understood the pressures on working women and families would surely guarantee a politics where some of those concerns found a voice.

The MPs themselves repeated widely that this was going to make a huge difference; that women's priorities would be on the agenda; that politics were going to be nicer for ever more. But there was something exceptionally bland and unconvincing about this. What exactly did the increase in the number of women signify apart from a sort of miasma of collective niceness which was supposed to spread throughout society? Would the gender of these women really make a difference to their policies and behaviour? It hadn't affected Margaret Thatcher. And when early in 1998 only five of these women voted against proposals to cut the lone-parent benefit, cynicism seemed well justified.

Apologists for the government rushed to its defence. Though the cuts would mainly affect women, they insisted that women's interests were being kept in mind all the time in formulating a new deal on benefits. And the budget of April 1998 was widely

217

called a women's budget. Behind all these arguments lay the oldest feminist conviction of them all: that an equal place in the labour market is the way to hand self-respect to women. Yet if we do take seriously the idea of real social and economic change, we do really now know in a clear way what women's interests are? Is this kind of language still relevant? Or is it the fixed belief of a group of professional women? In a society where men have been taking a bashing, do we really want the sort of feminism that insists on a woman's right to claim an equal place in the world of male power, that insists on women's lists, on promoting women's representation in Parliament, business and the upper echelons of society, and then does little to help the disadvantaged? It is one thing to demand rights when a whole group is clearly disadvantaged, but it is quite another if those rights seem mainly to confer additional advantages on already privileged groups, or groups who may be using women's interests to promote their own careers or their own agenda.

Of course, that's the nub of this book. What is really going on? Do we take the changes seriously or put them down as the birthpangs of a new order? If it is simply a matter of teething troubles, then the fact that men appear to be losing advantages in these social upheavals while women appear to be gaining ground is not the responsibility of feminists. Nor would it necessarily be a bad thing. Sean French has said that we may just have to accept that there will be a lost generation of men, the casualties of a period of adjustment, just as there was a period of pre-feminist women who never fulfilled their potential (*Guardian*, 12 May 1998). This loss would be no bad thing. Purely on the grounds of formal equality, women would still have to fight to achieve what would not be given otherwise.

But what if this sexual adjustment between the sexes is intersecting with an evolving and raw political and social situation, so that the rhetoric of rights, equalities and affirmative action to achieve them sometimes grates rancorously in a society which on the one hand is increasingly divided and on the other is more unsettled domestically. What if it turned out that we are not talking about a lost generation of men but of a rhetoric which is denying those men the chance to change?

In this book I have been arguing both that the meaning of gender division has undergone incredible changes and that feminist rhetoric has sometimes been used to bash disadvantaged men and boys. If that is so, it may be time to reconsider whether we want to continue special pleading for women's interests or defending women's 'rights' as greater or more pressing than men's. Obviously it would be necessary to prevent discrimination along gender lines, but would it not be more helpful to be looking at human rights and at the rights of all members of society?

The real aims now should be to be aware of gender division and how it can discriminate and to find policies which aim at equal treatment rather than to assume one sex or the other necessarily has advantages. We need to understand how people are living their lives and making their choices without preconceptions about men being one thing and women another. More than anything else, we must make sure that we are not dealing with passé notions of women's rights but with what is now right for all members of our society.

Alther, L., *Kinflicks*. London: Penguin, 1976.

Benn, M., *Madonna and Child*. London: Viking, 1997.

Blenkenhorn, D., *Fatherless America*. New York: Basic Books, 1995.

Bly, R., *Iron John*. New York: Addison-Wesley, 1990.

—— *Sibling Society*. London: Penguin, 1997.

Burgess, A., *Fatherhood Reclaimed: The Making of the Modern Family*. London: Vermilion, 1997.

Campbell, B., *Goliath: Britain's Dangerous Places*. London: 1993.

Chessler, P., *Women and Madness*. London: Allen Lane, 1972.

Coward, R., *Our Treacherous Hearts. Why Women Let Men Get Their Way*. London: Faber, 1992.

Coward, R. and Black, M., 'Linguistic, Sexual and Social Relations', in D. Cameron, *The Feminist Critique of Language*. London: Routledge, 1998.

Danziger, N., *Danziger's Britain: A Journey to the Edge*, London: Flamingo, 1997.

Demos Report, *No Turning Back: Generations and the Gender Quake*. London: Demos, 1995.

—— *Freedom's Children*. London: Demos, 1995.

—— *Tomorrow's Women*. London: Demos, 1997.

Dench, G., *Rewriting the Sexual Contract*. London: Institute of Community Studies, 1998.

Dennis, Norman and George Erdos, *Fatherless Families*. London: Institute of Economic Affairs, 1992.

Evans, M., *Introducing Contemporary Feminist Thought*. London: Polity Press, 1997.

Faludi, S., *Backlash: The Undeclared War against American Women*. New York: Crown, 1991.

Farrell, W., *The Myth of Male Power.* London: Fourth Estate, 1994.

French, M., *The Women's Room.* New York: Summit Books, 1977.

Friedan, B., *The Feminine Mystique,* New York: W. W. Norton, 1963.

Garner, H., *The First Stone.* London: Bloomsbury, 1997.

Grant, L., 'Sex and the Single Student' in *The War of the Words,* ed. Dunant, S. London: Virago, 1994.

Gray, J., *False Dawn. The Delusions of Global Capitalism.* London: Granta, 1998.

Hakim, K., 'The Sexual Division of Labour and Women's Heterogeneity', *British Journal of Sociology,* no. 47, 1996.

—— 'The Myth of Rising Female Employment', *Work Employment and Society,* no. 7, 1993.

Harman, H., *The Century Gap.* London: Vermilion, 1993.

Hill, D., *The Future of Men.* London: Weidenfeld and Nicolson, 1997.

Horlick, N., *Can You Have It All? (How to Succeed in a Man's World).* London: Macmillan, 1997.

Hutton, W., *The State We're In,* London: Jonathan Cape, 1996.

Jong, E., *Fear of Flying.* New York: Holt, Reinhardt and Winston, 1971.

Joshi, H. and Dex, S., 'Career and Motherhood in the 1990s', *Economic Policy Journal,* 1998.

Kraemer, S., *Active Fathering for the Future.* London: Demos, 1995.

Lees, S., *Carnal Knowledge.* London: Penguin, 1997.

Lyndon, N., *No More Sex War: The Failures of Feminism.* London: Mandarin, 1993.

McFerran, A., *Motherland.* London: Virago, 1998.

MacInnes, J., *The End of Masculinity.* Milton Keynes: Open University Press, 1997.

Millett, K., *Sexual Politics.* London: Abacus, 1970.

Mitchell, S., *Icons Saints and Divas,* London: Pandora, 1997.

Moore, S. (ed.), *Head Over Heels.* London: Viking, 1996.

Morgan, R., *Sisterhood is Powerful: An Anthology of Writings from the Women's Liberation Movement.* New York: Vintage, 1970.

Morrison, B., *As If.* London: Granta, 1997.

Mort, F., *Cultures of Consumption.* London: Routledge, 1996.

221

Oakley, A. and Mitchell, J. (eds), *Who's Afraid of Feminism?* London: Hamish Hamilton, 1997.

Pahl, R., *After Success*, London: Polity Press, 1995.

Phillips, M., *The Sex Change State*. London: Social Market Foundation, 1997.

Phillips, R., *Mapping, Men and Empire*. London: Routledge, 1997.

Roberts, Y., *Mad About Women*. London: Virago, 1993.

Roiphe, K., *The Morning After*. London: Hamish Hamilton, 1993.

Rowbotham, S., *Hidden From History*. London: Pluto, 1974.

Samuels, A., 'Segmentation and Synergy', in K. Scull (ed.), *Men, Work and Family*. Tarcher, 1992.

—— *The Good Enough Parent of Either Sex*. Unpublished paper, 1995.

Segal, L., *Slow Motion*. London: Virago, 1992.

Seidler, V., *Man Enough*, London: Sage, 1998.

Steinem, G., *Revolution from Within*. Boston: Little, Brown and Co., 1992.

Thomas, D., *Not Guilty: In Defence of Modern Man*. London: Weidenfeld and Nicolson, 1993.

Townsend, K., *Manhood at Harvard*. New York: Norton, 1997.

Valian, V., *Why So Slow?* MIT Press, 1998.

Walter, N., *The New Feminism*. London: Little, Brown and Co., 1998.

Wandor, M. (ed.), *Once a Feminist*. London: Virago, 1990.

Winship, J., 'Magazines for Girls', in R. Betterton, *Looking On*. London: Pandora, 1987.

INDEX